The Scott, Foresman PROCOM Series

Series Editors

Roderick P. Hart
University of Texas at Austin

Ronald L. Applbaum
Pan American University

Titles in the PROCOM Series

BETTER WRITING FOR PROFESSIONALS
A Concise Guide
Carol Gelderman

BETWEEN YOU AND ME
The Professional's Guide to Interpersonal Communication
Robert Hopper
In consultation with Lillian Davis

COMMUNICATION STRATEGIES FOR TRIAL ATTORNEYS
K. Phillip Taylor
Raymond W. Buchanan
David U. Strawn

THE CORPORATE MANAGER'S GUIDE TO BETTER COMMUNICATION
W. Charles Redding
In consultation with Michael Z. Sincoff

THE ENGINEER'S GUIDE TO BETTER COMMUNICATION
Richard Arthur
In consultation with Volkmer Reichert

GETTING THE JOB DONE
A Guide to Better Communication for Office Staff
Bonnie M. Johnson
In consultation with Geri Sherman

THE GUIDE TO BETTER COMMUNICATION IN GOVERNMENT SERVICE
Raymond L. Falcione
In consultation with James G. Dalton

THE MILITARY OFFICER'S GUIDE TO BETTER COMMUNICATION
L. Brooks Hill
In consultation with Major Michael Gallagher

THE NURSE'S GUIDE TO BETTER COMMUNICATION
Robert E. Carlson
In consultation with Margaret Kidwell Udin
and Mary Carlson

THE PHYSICIAN'S GUIDE TO BETTER COMMUNICATION
Barbara F. Sharf
In consultation with Dr. Joseph A. Flaherty

THE POLICE OFFICER'S GUIDE TO BETTER COMMUNICATION
T. Richard Cheatham
Keith V. Erickson
In consultation with Frank Dyson

PROFESSIONALLY SPEAKING
A Concise Guide
Robert Doolittle
In consultation with Thomas Towers

For further information, write to

Professional Publishing Group
Scott, Foresman and Company
1900 East Lake Avenue
Glenview, IL 60025

The Guide to Better Communication in Government Service

Raymond L. Falcione, Ph.D.
University of Maryland

in consultation with
James G. Dalton
National Society of Professional Engineers

Scott, Foresman and Company   Glenview, Illinois
Dallas, Texas   Oakland, New Jersey   Palo Alto, California
Tucker, Georgia   London

093814

For Dorcas, Raymond, Joseph, and Aaron

14, From COMMUNICATION AND ORGANIZATIONAL BEHAVIOR: *Text and Cases,* Third Edition, by William V. Haney, PH.D. Copyright © 1973 by Richard D. Irwin, Inc. Reprinted by permission; **19,** Photographs from *Nonverbal Communication Systems* by Dale G. Leathers, published by Allyn and Bacon, Inc., Boston, MA. Reprinted by permission of the author; **43,** From HUMAN RELATIONS AT WORK: THE DYNAMICS OF ORGANIZATIONAL BEHAVIOR, Third Edition, by Keith Davis, Ph.D. Copyright © 1967 by McGraw-Hill, Inc. Reprinted by permission.

Library of Congress Cataloging in Publication Data

Falcione, Raymond L.
   The guide to better communication in government service.

   Bibliography.
   Includes index.
   1. Communication in public administration. I. Dalton, James G. II. Title.
JF1525.C59F34 1984   350.007   83-20407
ISBN 0-673-15565-X (pbk.)

CONTENTS

CHAPTER *3*

Communication and Managing Others   51

CHAPTER *4*

Running Effective Meetings   79

CHAPTER *5*

Public and Interagency Communication in the Government   92

CHAPTER 6

Communication, Productivity, and the Future of Government Service 103

FOREWORD

This volume is part of a series entitled *ProCom* (Professional Communication), which has been created to bring the very latest thinking about human communication to the attention of working professionals. Busy professionals rarely have time for theoretical writings on communication oriented toward general readers, and the books in the ProCom series have been designed to provide the information they need. This volume and the others in the series focus on what communication scholars have learned recently that might prove useful to professionals, how certain principles of interaction can be applied in concrete situations, and what difference the latest thoughts about communication can make in the lives and careers of professionals.

Most professionals want to improve their communication skills in the context of their unique professional callings. They don't want pie-in-the-sky solutions divorced from the reality of their jobs. And, because they are professionals, they typically distrust uninformed advice offered by uninformed advisors, no matter how well intentioned the advice and the advisors might be.

The books in this series have been carefully adapted to the needs and special circumstances of modern professionals. For example, it becomes obvious that the skills needed by a nurse when communicating with the family of a terminally ill patient will differ markedly from those demanded of an attorney when coaxing crucial testimony out of a reluctant witness. Furthermore, analyzing the nurse's or attorney's experiences will hardly help an engineer explain a new bridge's stress fractures to state legislators, a military officer motivate a group of especially dispirited recruits, or a police officer calm a vicious domestic disturbance. All these situations require a special kind of professional with a special kind of professional training. It is ProCom's intention to supplement that training in the area of communication skills.

Each of the authors of the ProCom volumes has extensively taught, written about, and listened to professionals in his or her area. In addition, the books have profited from the services of area consultants—working professionals who have practical experience with the special kinds of communication problems that confront their co-workers. The authors and the area consultants have collaborated to provide solutions to these vexing problems.

We, the editors of the series, believe that ProCom will treat you well. We believe that you will find no theory-for-the sake-of-theory here. We believe that you will find a sense of expertise. We believe that you will find the content of the ProCom volumes to be specific rather than general, concrete rather than abstract, applied rather than theoretical. We believe that you will find the examples interesting, the information appropriate, and the applications useful. We believe that you will find the ProCom volumes helpful whether you read them on your own or use them in a workshop. We know that ProCom has brought together the most informed authors and the best analysis and advice possible. We ask you to add your own professional goals and practical experiences so that your human communication holds all the warmth that makes it human and all the clarity that makes it communication.

Roderick P. Hart
University of Texas at Austin

Ronald L. Applbaum
Pan American University

PREFACE

Like all organizations, government is a network of people who are trying to get work done in pursuit of a particular mission. In the case of the federal, state, and local government, that "work" is all-encompassing. It is the nation's business on the one hand, and little more than answering routine telephone calls about drivers license renewal on the other. But no matter what the work, getting it done requires communication.

Communication in federal, state, and local government is what this book is about. It provides some helpful suggestions for communicating more effectively. It is written with you, the manager, specifically in mind, and for a very good reason. As a manager, you have a particular communication responsibility. You face special kinds of problems because your job has an added communication dimension. Not only must you be concerned about the jobs your units do, and about the internal flow of communication among the various people doing them, you must also be concerned about these things as they relate to matters of policy, political concerns and other public considerations. Not only must you communicate, you must also supervise and make effective the communication process itself within the government fishbowl.

This book begins by orienting you to the broad context of government and the general principles that govern all communication (Chapter 1). From that point, the communication processes within government agencies are examined in some detail, with particular attention being paid to issues of credibility, motivation, and leadership (Chapter 2). A generic communication model that you can adapt to your own context to help you counsel and coach your employees is presented in Chapter 3. Chapters 4 and 5 help you conduct more effective meetings and briefings. In the final chapter, we take a brief look at some successful communication attempts within government programs, and at what makes them successful. A rating chart is included at the end of the book to help you launch your own "communication audit" as you begin to implement the learning you have gained from the book.

In my opinion, you, the government manager, have not been given the credit you deserve. My own experience has told me that you are dedicated professionals who want to do the best job you can. Hopefully, this book will help you communicate more effectively in what is the largest organization in the world—Government.

ACKNOWLEDGMENTS

I would like to thank Doris Moore, Mirco Snidero, and Blair Ewing for their helpful comments during interviews and their insight into the workings of federal government. I would also like to thank James G. Dalton for his helpful thoughts in putting this volume together.

RLF

CHAPTER 7

The Realities of Working for the Government: Organization and Communication Basics

MEMO

TO: Reader
FR: Author
RE: Chapter 1

This chapter reviews the realities of working for government agencies and some basic communication principles which affect your job. You'll be exploring the following topics:

1. Characteristics of government organizations
2. Political appointees and career civil servants
3. Government organizations and information flow
4. The importance of redundancy
5. Types and purposes of messages
6. Five basic laws of communication
7. Nonverbal communication

During a recent conference on productivity in Washington, D.C., I heard a presentation by the former assistant director of Productivity Programs at the Office of Personnel Management (OPM). The speaker made it very clear that the public still perceives government workers as low risk takers, sometimes as wasteful and corrupt, often as inefficient and ineffective. While these perceptions aren't accurate, they are still realities because the public acts on them. The speaker went on to say that government must change—and prove it has changed—under conditions of limited resources, high inflation, and smaller government bureaucracy.

The presentation reflected a growing philosophy of government, one that emphasizes a much leaner bureaucracy that does "more with less." This philosophy requires a more efficient and effective use of people and resources. Most importantly, this new way of looking at government carries a communication imperative: you as managers must communicate effectively, particularly on interpersonal and group levels.

During the last ten years as a communication professor and consultant, I have concluded, not surprisingly, that the single most important skill managers possess is the ability to communicate effectively up and down the organizational hierarchy. As a government manager, don't ever forget that to many of your subordinates, you *are* the organization. Whether you like it or not, you are a *walking message*, and even though your subordinates don't evaluate your performance, they evaluate you constantly on the basis of those messages conveyed through your communication behavior.

The purpose of this book is to help you, the government manager, to become a more effective communicator in a system that is under constant scrutiny and constant pressure to produce; it experiences constant ambiguity over what its *product* is; it is under constant pressure to produce more, with less.

When we talk about the federal bureaucracy and many state governments, we are talking about some of the largest organizations in the United States. For example, there are approximately three million government employees and nearly three thousand political appointees in the federal service. Figure 1.1 shows how vast the federal government is.

CHARACTERISTICS OF GOVERNMENT ORGANIZATIONS

A number of factors combine to give government organizations a distinctive set of characteristics that set them apart from organizations in the private sector. One of the most obvious differences is the nature of the product or service rendered. Success or failure of an organization in the private sector depends on whether it survives in the marketplace, which is

FIGURE 1.1   The Government of the United States

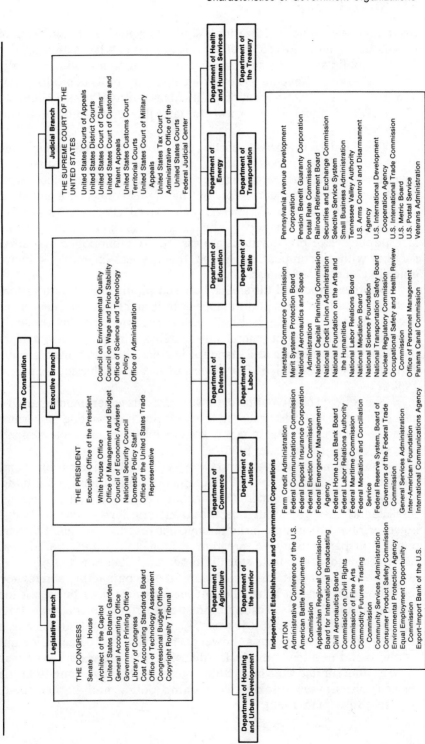

based, in turn, on the organization's ability to generate enough revenue to exceed its expenditures for product development, advertising, sales, etc. But the public sector doesn't necessarily deal with a product; usually it provides services. Revenue is not generated on the basis of product quality and customer satisfaction, but on political feasibility (Pursley & Snortland 1980). Where there is a power to tax, the profit motive becomes unnecessary.

Thus, unlike the private sector, the public-sector consumer doesn't always define the market (Pursley & Snortland 1980). In reality, the government's customers are program recipients, and the product or service is not defined by the marketplace but by the marketeer, the government agency, and hence by the Congress. In other words, the public sector is not as dependent on the demands of the marketplace as the private sector. In fact, public-sector organizations are essentially monopolies that provide services without competition. Hence, there is less incentive to increase efficiency and effectiveness.

Another important difference between public and private sectors is that, historically at least, performance criteria and standards have been far less apparent in the public sector. Criteria such as return on investment and earnings per share are not generally measurable in the public sector. Nor are the performance criteria and standard business uses to measure success and failure easily established for government service (Pursley & Snortland 1980).

The concept of separation of powers also sets government apart. It can generate mistrust—and guarded communication—among government agencies because of the inherent responsibility to balance competing interest groups (Silberman 1980).

The separation of salary and expense (S & E) budgets from program budgets is also characteristic of government organizations. S & E budgets are reviewed and administered independently, and are often thoroughly dissected as they go through each bureaucratic level. Program budgets, however, often go through the heirarchy unchanged. Consequently, there is often a disparity between program responsibility and the necessary resources needed to administer the program (Silberman 1980).

The four year political cycle insures the accountability and review of the nation's leadership. When the four years are nearly up, the public looks at the accomplishments of each administration in relation to the goals it set and decides how successful it was. This is a significant attribute of our democratic process. It tends, however, to create the demand for quick solutions and politically motivated decisions that are visible. As a result, there is often limited time to do things correctly, based on long-term goals. Instead, short-range thinking concerning policy and implementation persists (Silberman 1980).

POLITICAL APPOINTEES AND CAREER CIVIL SERVANTS

Another result of the political cycle is the division it may create between political appointees and career civil servants. Often the political appointees are doing temporary duty. They spend approximately four years in government service and seldom stay long enough to experience the full consequences of their decisions. The average tenure of an assistant secretary, for example, is about eighteen months. This makes the relationship between the career civil servant and the political appointee very tenuous, to say the least.

An example of the tenuousness of this relationship occurred to me in 1976. Two other professors and I were hired by a government agency to develop an extensive management program. One consultant was responsible for a training program in motivation principles, the other for a program in problem solving. My responsibility was to develop a program of generic communication skills that could apply to both motivation and problem solving. The three of us worked for five and a half months and finished the entire program, including participant and trainer manuals and video tape models.

The agency representatives had expressed a real desire to get the pilot program underway before the November elections. They were fearful that a new administration would cancel the program. But for some unknown reason, the pilot program was postponed until after Jimmy Carter was elected. It wasn't long before "heads began to roll," with people leaving the agency almost daily. The program, which had cost a great deal of money, was scrapped. When I asked a career civil servant what had happened, he said, "Simple. The program didn't have the new administration's stamp on it. If it's not their baby, they don't want it. The only chance we had to get it on board was to have seen that damn pilot program. Then the momentum would have carried it forward. Now it's canned."

The communication relevance to this is clear. The kind of mistrust that defeats program continuity between administrations can only be checked through better communication between career civil servants and political appointees.

So we can see there are some fundamental differences between private and public sector organizations: the former generally provides a product, based on quality and profit motive, while the latter provides a service, based on political feasibility, and there is no profit motive. The performance criteria, budget procedures, political cycles, and temporary appointees are areas which represent differences between private- and public-sector organizations. These differences present government managers with unique challenges in motivating and communicating with employees. Let's take a look at some of the problems government organizations have with communication.

GOVERNMENT ORGANIZATIONS AND INFORMATION FLOW

As organizations grow larger, communication problems grow with them. As a member of the largest bureaucracy in the Western world, you've experienced problems such as information overload/underload, lack of coordination, lack of innovation, increased formality, heavy emphasis on rules and regulations, inflexibility, and dissatisfaction. In a recent review of sixteen different organizations (Goldhaber et al. 1977), government organizations made a poor showing compared to other private-sector organizations on four grounds:

1. Employees in government organizations expressed a greater need to receive more information in areas such as job duties, how well they are doing on the job, how they are being judged, how job-related problems are being handled, and how their job relates to the total organization.

2. Employees in government organizations expressed a greater need for more information about what they are doing on their jobs, what they think the job requirements are, job-related problems, complaints about the job, evaluation of their supervisor's performance, and clearer work instructions.

3. Government employees expressed a greater need to receive more information from such sources as middle management, top management, department meetings, and formal management presentations.

4. Government employees tended to be less satisfied with their progress, their chances for upward mobility, the opportunity to make a difference, the organization's system for recognizing and rewarding outstanding performance, the organization's concern for their welfare, overall communication efforts, and the organization's ability to achieve its goals and objectives.

As organizations increase in size so do the number of levels information must flow through. As these levels increase, so does the likelihood for distortion. We've all played the telephone game when we were in elementary school. A message is transmitted down the line from one child to another, and by the time the message reaches the last child, it is completely distorted. This also happens in organizations, as the following example shows:

Operation Halley's Comet

A Colonel issued the following directive to his executive officers: "Tomorrow evening at approximately 2000 hours Halley's Comet will be visible in this area, an event which occurs only once every seventy-five years. Have the men fall out in the battalion area in fatigues, and I will explain this rare phenomenon to them. In case of rain, we will not be able to see anything, so assemble the men in the theater and I will show them films of it."

Executive Officer to Company Commander: "By order of the Colonel, tomorrow at 2000 hours, Halley's Comet will appear above the battalion area. If it rains, fall the men out in fatigues, then march to the theater where the rare phenomenon will take place, something which occurs only once every seventy-five years."

Company Commander to Lieutenant: "By order of the Colonel in fatigues at 2000 hours tomorrow evening, the phenomenal Halley's Comet will appear in the theater. In case of rain, in the battalion area, the Colonel will give another order, something which occurs once every seventy-five years."

Lieutenant to Sergeant: "Tomorrow at 2000 hours, the Colonel will appear in the theater with Halley's Comet, something which happens every seventy-five years, if it rains. The Colonel will order the Comet into the battalion area."

Sergeant to Squad: "When it rains tomorrow at 2000 hours, the phenomenal seventy-five-year-old General Halley, accompanied by the Colonel, will drive his Comet through the battalion area theater in fatigues."

It is generally safe to assume that as information is communicated serially from one level to another, it will be distorted, and this could become a major problem. There is, however, a way of avoiding the problem, —be redundant.

THE IMPORTANCE OF REDUNDANCY

We often assume we have communicated sufficiently when we send messages to others, only to find out later that our message was significantly distorted. One way to counter this problem is to develop redundant or backup message systems. Just as the space shuttle has backup computers (redundant mechanisms) to make sure it will land safely, you can use backup procedures when you transmit information. These backup procedures increase in importance as the organization increases in size.

Rule of Thumb #1   Whenever you send an important message to someone orally, back it up with a written memo; whenever you send an important memo to someone, back it up orally. Obviously you use your own discretion about how often and under what conditions to do this because it does take time and energy. If you look at the process from a time perspective, it does reduce your *efficiency*. But it will often increase your *effectiveness* by reducing misunderstanding.

   Rule of Thumb #2   After giving someone instructions about something, try not to ask, "Do you understand?" There is often considerable pressure on subordinates to say "yes" to such a question, whether there is understanding or not. An alternative way of asking a subordinate if he or she understands something might be, "I'm not sure if I was very clear. How do you understand the situation?" or "What steps are you going to follow on the project?" etc. In order to increase the likelihood of being understood, you can back up your written or oral message when necessary, and solicit feedback from the other person to insure understanding. These two small suggestions can save you a good deal of time and frustration in the long run. At this point, let's analyze the types and purposes of messages we send in the organization. It may give us some insight into our communication behavior.

TYPES AND PURPOSES OF MESSAGES

We all want our units to run smoothly and effectively. To do this, we must be able to take information and transform it into clear messages for the people who work for us. One way to better understand how this is done is to classify messages into catergories, such as shown in Table 1.1.

TABLE 1.1   *Types of Messages*

Message Type	Definition	Example
Task	Concerned with the products, services, and activities of specific interest to the organization	Operating procedures; Reports; Task orientation; Manuals
Maintenance	Concerned with policy and regulations of the organization	Annual planning sessions; Goal statements; Position papers; Orders
Human	Concerned with the people in the organization, taking into account their feelings, relationship, satisfaction, etc.	Performance appraisals; Performance awards; Counseling sessions; Social activities
Innovative	Concerned with responding to environmental change and new ideas	New programs; Task forces; Strategic planning sessions; Suggestion systems

Table 1.1 is based on categories suggested by Goldhaber (1979).

A positive relationship exists between the sufficient communication of these message types and employee satisfaction and performance.

One way to look at the above message types as they relate to your organization and employees is illustrated in Figure 1.2.

FIGURE 1.2 How Messages Relate to Organizations

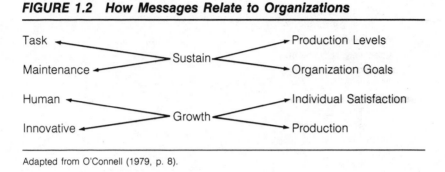

Adapted from O'Connell (1979, p. 8).

Let's take a few moments to examine your unit's communication needs by assessing each of the message types.

Self-Assessment of Your Use of Message Types

Indicate the degree to which you do the following:

Task	Very Little	Little	Some	Great	Very Great
Give clear instructions concerning job tasks					
Give timely task information					
Give accurate, up-to-date task information					
Clearly explain policies and procedures to employees					
Maintenance					
Conduct effective problem-solving meetings					
Conduct effective information-giving meetings					
Clearly communicate the goals and direction of the department or unit					

	Very Little	Little	Some	Great	Very Great
Conduct annual planning sessions for the department or unit	_____	_____	_____	_____	_____

Human

Conduct effective participative performance appraisals	_____	_____	_____	_____	_____
Effectively counsel employees in career development	_____	_____	_____	_____	_____
Effectively orient new employees to the responsibilities, procedures, policies of the organization, department, or unit	_____	_____	_____	_____	_____
Give quick, positive feedback for good performance	_____	_____	_____	_____	_____

Innovative

Provide a climate where suggestions and/or complaints are free to be aired	_____	_____	_____	_____	_____
Solicit questions and ideas from employees	_____	_____	_____	_____	_____
Accept all ideas or suggestions as useful or potentially useful	_____	_____	_____	_____	_____
Conduct periodic brainstorming and planning sessions					

After you've completed the assessment instrument, go back and check the items you marked "Little" or "Very Little." These are the areas which need some improvement. This instrument is designed to give you valuable feedback on the messages you convey in your organization.

FIVE BASIC LAWS OF COMMUNICATION

Regardless of how you assess your communication behavior regarding the message types, there are communication principles that will always affect your managerial effectiveness. In this section, we will look at certain *communication laws* that invariably affect your ability to deal effectively with people in the organization.

Law 1   *You Cannot Not Communicate*   As stated earlier in this chapter, we are all walking messages. It is not a question of communicating or not communicating, it is a matter of what level we are communicating on. The first is the *intrapersonal level*, the communication that takes place internally. It consists of the relationship we have with our environment. It takes form in the attitudes, values, beliefs, and internal reactions we have toward all kinds of stimuli existing in our surroundings.

The second level is the *interpersonal level* on a one-to-one basis. In our daily interpersonal situations with our bosses, co-workers, and subordinates, all behavior, verbal and nonverbal, has some message value. (Nonverbal communication will be considered separately, later in the chapter.)

The third level is the *small group*. The communication which occurs in small groups is obviously interpersonal in nature, but because small groups possess some formal structure and purpose, it is more appropriate to classify them as a distinct level.

The fourth level is the *organizational communication level*, which consists of the interdependent relationships of interpersonal and group communication as they move toward larger system goals. It is the formal and informal processes which take place within an organizational system that help the system achieve its objectives.

Public communication is the fifth level. As managers we are often asked to address others, formally or informally, in public presentations and briefings. For many, public communication is more difficult than the other levels because it requires careful preparation, enthusiasm, composure, and a sensitivity to the feedback inherent in a public setting. (Public communication will be considered in more detail in Chapter 5.)

To view communication as a one-way linear transmission of messages from one place to another is far from accurate. Communication is an ongoing process; we are always communicating at some level.

Law 2   *Information Is Potentially Power*   Max Weber, often called the "Father of Bureaucracy," said that the civil servant's power was vested in the legality of the office held. He felt this was one of the primary criteria determining whether a person has power to influence behavior in organizations. A member of any modern organization realizes, however, that legal authority is not the only factor that gives power. In addition to the formal network, there is an informal network operating in all organizations, and the leaders of this informal network influence others greatly. These informal leaders may never appear on the traditional organizational charts because they possess little or no legal authority. But they are *gatekeepers* nevertheless, because they control a great deal of the information flow. And because they control the information flow, they are more able to influence the behavior of others.

Secretaries are an excellent example of such gatekeepers. They are often the people we go to when we want to tap into grapevine information, as well as to find out about formal policy. You won't see secretaries on an organizational chart, but they often influence organizations greatly because they control information. Consider the following humorous description of the federal bureaucracy.

The President

Leaps tall buildings in a single bound
Is more powerful than a locomotive
Is faster than a speeding bullet
Walks on water
Gives policy to God

The Vice President

Leaps short buildings in a single bound
Is more powerful than a switch engine
Is just as fast as a speeding bullet
Talks with God

Cabinet Member

Leaps short buildings with a running
    start and favorable winds
Is almost as powerful as a switch engine
Is faster than a speeding BB
Walks on water in an indoor swimming pool
Talks with God if a special request is honored

Agency Director

Barely clears a Quonset hut
Loses tug of war with a locomotive
Can fire a speeding bullet
Swims well
Is occasionally addressed by God

Deputy Director

Makes high marks on the walls when
    trying to leap tall buildings
Is run over by locomotives
Can sometimes handle a gun without
    inflicting self-injury
Treads water
Talks to animals

Division Director

Climbs walls continually
Rides the rails
Plays Russian roulette
Walks on thin ice
Prays a lot

Branch Head

Runs into buildings
Recognizes locomotives two out of three times
Is not issued ammunition
Can stay afloat with a life jacket
Talks to walls

Section Head

Falls over doorstep when trying to
    enter buildings
Says "Look at the choo-choo"
Wets himself with a water pistol
Plays in mud puddles
Mumbles to himself

Secretary

Lifts buildings and walks under them
Kicks locomotives off the tracks
Catches speeding bullets in her teeth
    and eats them
Freezes water with a single glance
She is God

Law 3 Words Have No Meaning The term *meaning* can be understood two ways: as *connotative*, or associative meaning, and as *denotative*, or operational meaning. Denotative meanings are basically dictionary definitions, the agreed-upon meanings attributed to words in our culture. Although a word may have a fairly stable meaning, that does not eliminate problems for people who use the word because nearly all words have multiple usage. The average educated adult in this country uses about two thousand words in daily interaction, and the five hundred most commonly used words have over fourteen thousand dictionary definitions! (Berman 1965.)

Since we don't normally carry Webster's in our hip pockets, we usually deal with others on the level of connotative meaning. These are the thoughts, feelings, or perceptions that we have about a word. And, since we are all different, we will always bring differing degrees of meaning to a word no matter what the word may be. Many of our most familiar words are abundant with connotative meaning—mother, president, religion, happiness, love, success, bureaucracy, etc. It is important to realize that, as words become more abstract, the more difficult it is to achieve mutually agreed upon meaning.

The word is not the thing. It only represents the thing. Virtually all words have denotative and connotative meaning. The type and degree of reaction that humans give to words will vary from one person to another. Meanings reside not in the words, but in the minds of those who use them or are exposed to them.

We've all been guilty of, or at least exposed to, the *bureaucratese* which has become so common. Look at the following three columns for a moment and match any three words from the three columns and see what you come up with. The three words chosen may not make sense, but I bet they will be at their bureaucratese best (Haney 1979).

Column 1	Column 2	Column 3
0. Integrated	0. Management	0. Options
1. Total	1. Organizational	1. Flexibility
2. Systematized	2. Monitored	2. Capability
3. Parallel	3. Reciprocal	3. Mobility
4. Functional	4. Digital	4. Programming
5. Responsive	5. Logic	5. Concept
6. Optical	6. Transitional	6. Time-phase
7. Synchronized	7. Incremental	7. Projection
8. Compatible	8. Third-generation	8. Hardware
9. Balanced	9. Policy	9. Contingency

Law 4   The Greater the Need to Communicate, the More Difficult It Becomes   This law of communication may well be the human dilemma! Let's look at what it says a bit more closely. Whenever we have problems in our relationships it's usually because we aren't communicating very effectively with each other. We know that it's becoming increasingly necessary to confront the issues and deal with them. We also know we should say to the other person, "Let's sit down and talk about the problem." Ironically, as the need to discuss problems increases, so does the difficulty to do it! As humans, we sometimes forget that the need and the difficulty to communicate are often synonymous because our emotions, biases, and perceptions all get in the way of our ability to deal with the issues rationally. How many of us have subordinates or bosses with whom we have real communication problems? Over time, unless the problems are confronted, we develop numerous perceptions which invariably become distorted and minimize our ability to discuss the problem rationally. Consequently, there is the tendency to avoid one another if possible, or to have our periodic flare-ups, or to allow our anger to spill over into our other relationships. Later on in this book we'll look at some very specific techniques to help us deal more effectively with situations such as these.

Law 5 The Nature of a Relationship Is Contingent Upon the Punctuation of the Communicational Sequence Between the Communi-cants How's that for a noncommunicative message about communication! Let me be redundant for a moment and try to explain another human dilemma. Just as we punctuate syllables in words to give them emphasis, we tend to punctuate events in order to give them emphasis as well. Where we punctuate or give emphasis to these events determines our reality about the event! I know that explanation doesn't help much, so let me be exceedingly redundant by citing a couple of examples: The husband nags because the wife withdraws—doesn't speak up, doesn't talk, doesn't whatever (husband's punctuation). On the other hand, the wife withdraws and doesn't speak because the husband nags (wife's punctuation). Now where is the reality of the event? The reality is in the minds of participants in the event. A parallel example occurs in organizations. The supervisor doesn't like the subordinate because he never speaks up in meetings and isn't a team player (supervisor's punctuation). The subordinate doesn't participate in meetings and doesn't feel a part of the team because, you guessed it, the supervisor doesn't like him (subordinate's punctuation).

We might take a minute to reflect on where and when we inappropriately punctuate events, and how those events have made us less effective communicators.

NONVERBAL COMMUNICATION

For just a moment I'd like to examine the following continuum ranging from 0 to 100 percent. Notice the word *meaning* above it.

Meaning

0 ——————————————— 100%

How much meaning, not necessarily understanding, but *meaning*—do you think we derive from our transactions with others on the basis of our nonverbal behavior? Most people respond with 30 percent or 50 percent. The research suggests very different conclusions. One researcher found approximately 90 percent of meaning derived in our social transactions is determined by nonverbal messages (Mehrabian 1971).

The research on nonverbal communication has been prolific in recent years. For our purpose, however, let's briefly look at four classifications of nonverbal communication which have particular relevance to organizational transactions. They are body language, distance, vocal intonation, and facial expressions.

Body Language

In organizations, our bodies communicate many messages, particularly about our status and interpersonal responsiveness.

Generally in our culture, individuals who possess a high degree of organizational authority tend to be more expansive and relaxed in the way they act, while individuals of lower authority or status tend to appear more attentive. Sometimes, particularly when the subordinate has a concern or problem to discuss, the supervisor's expansive posture can unintentionally convey a detachment or lack of concern for the subordinate. *Rule of Thumb:* When someone expresses concern over a problem, *lean forward* in your chair, maintain good *frontal eye contact* with the person, and *attend* to what is being said by nodding and reinforcing audibly with such phrases as "go on," "when," "where," etc.

Managers often underestimate their ability to influence others by their nonverbal behavior. The behavior we exhibit by our bodies can unintentionally influence the perception of empathy dramatically. Remember, we judge ourselves on the basis of our *intentions*, but others judge us on the basis of our *behavior*. No matter what we intend to convey to our subordinates, if our nonverbal behavior is incongruent with what we say verbally—you can bet on it—the subordinate will believe what is seen, not what is heard.

By way of illustration of this point, when I was a graduate student, I used to have periodic meetings with my advisor. During those meetings, he would nervously tap his foot as he sat. I found myself cutting off numerous conversations with him because his foot-tapping "meant" he didn't have much time to talk. He would say, "Come in, Ray, what's on your mind?" foot-tapping away! I would often start our conversation by saying, "I know you're busy, I'll only be a minute." Verbally he always had time for me; nonverbally, he didn't. Finally, I mustered the courage to comment on my feelings, and said that I got the feeling he was very busy and found it difficult to take the time to talk. When he asked me what gave me that impression, my stomach churned as I said, "Well, it's, ah, your foot." He laughed, slapped his knee and said, "I just do that. It's idiosyncratic, I guess. Please don't let it bother you." The question is how many idiosyncratic behaviors do we have which might influence our subordinates' perceptions?

Distance

The distance we maintain between each other in our conversations will often define the nature of the relationship. In our culture, for example, touching to about eighteen inches is usually conducive to intimate relationships including whispers, secrets, etc.; eighteen inches to about four feet is more conducive to personal transactions such as those we have with friends and co-workers; four to twelve feet is usually conducive to more social transactions, such as those we have with subordinates, upper management, etc. We all carry with us a "bubble of personal space" that is essentially "culture bound." We all have our own comfort zones which, when invaded, can create real anxiety for us.

Again, a personal example will illustrate. When I first moved to the Washington, D.C., area, I attended a cocktail party, and was talking to a gentleman from Saudi Arabia. He talked very rapidly and very close to my face. I found myself nodding a great deal while backing up a little at a time—until he had backed me up against the wall! He was invading my comfort zone and I modified the distance between us as we talked. I finally smiled and said, "I have a difficult time talking this closely," and he responded by laughing and explaining that in his culture, "the feeling of breath on one's face is a sign of a good relationship." We tend to do two things when our personal space is invaded: we tend to maximize the tolerable distance between us, and minimize the degree of eye contact. (Test this out the next time you get into an elevator.)

Distance also pertains to the way we arrange our furniture and where we sit during certain transactions. For example, the desk and chair arrangement can affect a transaction. Sitting across from one another with a desk between you and the other person tends to be more conducive to formal, possibly even competitive transactions, while sitting side by side or at right angles is conducive to more informal, cooperative transactions. People also tend to feel more at ease and converse more with each other when they sit this way than they do sitting face-to-face across a table. How does the seating arrangement look in your office? Do you feel it helps or hinders the kinds of transactions you want to occur?

Rule of thumb If you want to formalize a transaction such as a discipline or employment interview, sit face-to-face with your desk between you and the other person. If you want to deformalize a transaction and increase the tendency to be cooperative, sit side by side or at right angles.

Vocal Intonation

"It's not always what we say, but how we say it." There's a good deal of truth to that statement. The tone, volume, and pitch of a person's voice can influence the meaning of the message significantly. While we can control the words we use, it's not as easy to control the way the words are spoken. Pauses, intonation, volume, etc., express our feelings much more clearly than the words themselves. The interesting thing is that, in cases where we have strong feelings about something, we usually can't mask the paralinguistic elements of our words very well. What's even more interesting is that people believe the paralinguistic part of the message more than the verbalized message. *Rule of Thumb:* Whenever there is a disparity between what we say and how we say it, people will believe how we said it and what they perceive the meaning to be, not what we said.

Facial Expressions

Another nonverbal element that affects our transactions significantly is our facial expression. Recently, Leathers (1976) developed the Facial Meaning Sensitivity Test (FMST) which allows people to identify the emotions of happiness, anger, surprise, sadness, disgust, and fear by observing pictures with various facial configurations. Take a look at the ten pictures in Figure 1.3 and try to match the corresponding emotions.

Eye contact may be the most important element of facial expressions. Goldhaber (1979) nicely summarizes some of the research findings:

1. Eye contact seems to occur under the following conditions
   a. When people seek feedback concerning the reaction of other people
   b. When an individual wants to signal that the communication channel is open
   c. When an individual wants to signal a need for affiliation, involvement, or inclusion
2. Women seem to engage in more eye contact in a variety of situations than do men
3. Eye contact seems to increase as the communicating pair increases the distance between themselves
4. Eye contact can be used to produce anxiety in others
5. Eye contact is absent under the following conditions
   a. When people want to hide their inner feelings
   b. When two parties are physically close to each other
   c. In competitive situations where there is dislike or tension, or after recent deception
   d. When a speaker begins a long utterance or when listeners anticipate a long, boring utterance
   e. When an individual wishes to disavow maintenance of all social contact

FIGURE 1.3 Facial Meaning Sensitivity Test (FMST)

Write the number of the photograph next to the emotion it best represents.

_____ Disgust	_____ Contempt
_____ Happiness	_____ Surprise
_____ Interest	_____ Anger
_____ Sadness	_____ Determination
_____ Bewilderment	_____ Fear

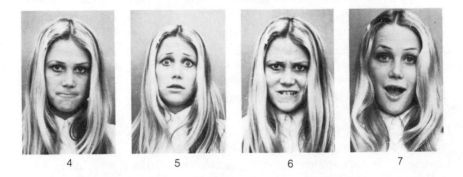
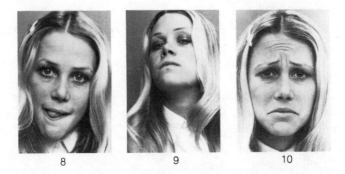

The correct answers for the FMST are as follows: (1) Disgust, (3) Happiness, (8) Interest, (10) Sadness, (2) Bewilderment, (9) Contempt, (7) Surprise, (6) Anger, (4) Determination, (5) Fear

A general word of caution should be emphasized before concluding this section on nonverbal communication. Don't attempt to interpret nonverbal behavior independent of the social and verbal context: they are interrelated. So the next time someone crosses his arms during a conversation with you don't draw any conclusions until you've thought of the social context, the relationship, and the verbalized message. After all, he could simply be more comfortable that way.

In summary, you, as managers, must never forget that you are indeed "walking messages." You are always communicating on some level whether you want to or not, and to your subordinates, you *are* the organization. Close attention to the messages you convey to your employees can help you achieve a higher level of effectiveness. Be sure to pay close attention to the basic laws of communication outlined in the chapter, and to become specifically aware of the significant communication value inherent in all nonverbal communication.

References

Berman, S. I. 1965. *Understanding and being understood.* San Diego, CA: The International Communication Institute. Brooks, W. 1971. *Speech Communications,* Dubuque, Iowa: William C. Brown.

Government Printing Office. 1980. *Federal Managers Guide to Washington.*

Goldhaber, G., D. Porter, & M. Yates. 1977. The ICA communication audit survey instrument: 1977 organizational norms. Paper presented at a meeting of the International Communication Association, Berlin, Germany.

Goldhaber, G. 1979. *Organizational communication.* Dubuque, Iowa: William C. Brown.

Haney, W. V. 1973. *Communication and organizational behavior: Text and cases.* 3d ed. Homewood, Illinois: Richard D. Irwin.

Leathers, D. B. 1976. *Nonverbal communications systems.* Boston: Allyn & Bacon.

Mehrabian, A. 1971. *Silent messages.* Belmont, CA: Wadsworth.

O'Connell, S. E. 1979. *The manager as communicator.* New York: Harper & Row.

Pursley, R. D. & N. Snortland. 1980. *Managing government organizations.* Mass: Wadsworth.

Silberman, H. S. 1980. Working in Washington. *Phi Delta Kappan.* 61: 445–49.

Watzlawick, P., J. H. Beavin, & D. D. Jackson. 1967. *The pragmatics of human communication.* New York: W. W. Norton & Co.

Communication Within the Government Agency

MEMO

TO: Reader
FR: Author
RE: Chapter 2

This chapter deals more specifically with communication within government agencies by covering both formal and informal communication as well as their impact on motivation and leadership effectiveness. You'll be exploring the following topics:

1. Written communication
2. Informal communication
3. Formal channels of communication
4. Communication climate
5. Communication climate inventory
6. Other factors influencing communication climate
7. Credibility profile
8. Improving your credibility
9. Motivation in government organizations
10. Characteristics that motivate
11. Leadership in government organizations

Every organization, regardless of its type, processes an incredible amount of written, verbal, and nonverbal communication. How effectively that communication is processed will determine management's success or failure in creating a healthy communication climate, motivating employees, and providing leadership.

The purpose of this chapter is to provide recommendations for   **21** increased effectiveness in your communication and management skills. Specifically, the chapter covers: (1) written communication skills that will help eliminate the affliction of bureaucratese; (2) informal communication and the grapevine; (3) formal communication channels; (4) the dimensions of a healthy communication climate; and (5) motivational and leadership principles that will help you increase your managerial effectiveness.

WRITTEN COMMUNICATION

Although this book is predominantly concerned with oral communication, written communication certainly needs mentioning, particularly because there is such an overwhelming emphasis on paperwork in government organizations.

. Let's look at four basic communication principles as they relate to writing:

Each recipient of a written message will interpret it according to his or her frame of reference.   Remembering the above statement can help us adapt our writing style and words to a particular audience. When we don't consider the frame of reference of our readers, we can cause unnecessary communication problems. Consider the following story. It's based on Murphy's law number ten, which states, "by making something absolutely clear, someone will become confused."

The Wayside Chapel

Background   An English lady was looking for a room while visiting Switzerland and asked the schoolmaster if he could recommend any. He took her to see several rooms and when everything was settled, the lady returned home to England to make the final preparations to go back to Switzerland. When she arrived home, the thought occurred to her that she didn't see a W.C. (water closet or toilet) anywhere around the place. So she immediately wrote a note to the schoolmaster asking him if there was a W.C. around. The schoolmaster was a poor pupil of English so he asked a parish priest if he could help in the matter. Together they tried to discover the meaning of the letters "W.C." and the only solution they could find for the letters was "Wayside Chapel." The schoolmaster then wrote the following note to the English lady:

Dear Madam:

I take pleasure in informing you that the W.C. is situated nine miles from the house in the center of a beautiful grove of pine trees, surrounded by lovely grounds. It is capable of holding 229 people and it is open on Sundays and Thursdays only. As there are a great number of people expected in the summer months, I would especially recommend that you come early, although there is plenty of standing room. This is an unfortunate situation if you are in the habit of going regularly.

You will be glad to hear that a good number of the people bring their own lunch and make a day of it while others who can afford a car, arrive just in time. I would recommend your Ladyship go on Thursdays when there will be an organ accompaniment. The acoustics are excellent and the most delicate sounds can be heard everywhere.

It may interest you to know that my daughter was married in the W.C. It was there that she met her husband. I can remember the rush there was for seats. There were two people in seats normally occupied by one. It was wonderful to see the expressions on the faces of those people. The newest attraction is a bell that rings every time someone enters. A bazaar is to be held to provide plush seats for all. My wife is rather delicate so she can't attend regularly. It is almost a year since she went. Naturally, it pains her very much not to be able to go more often.

I shall be delighted to reserve the best seats for you if you wish, where you will be seen by all. Hoping to be of some service to you.

The Schoolmaster

Writing is a one way linear transmission of a message which usually doesn't allow for immediate feedback. Because there is limited opportunity to immediately respond to written messages, feedback can create real problems in organizations. Here are four ways to generate feedback:

1. Use cover sheets on memoranda that ask the reader to evaluate the course of action recommended.
2. Install a telephone "Hot Line" system that enables readers to ask questions about a written document.
3. Check out readers' reactions orally (remember *redundancy* in Chapter 1).
4. Attach a list of follow-up actions to the written document and check the one action you would like to see taken by the reader.

Keep your writing simple and straightforward The following is a humorous example of "government prose" I heard in a speech presented by Charles Redding, a leading authority in organizational communication. He cited it as an example of writing that was far from being simple and straightforward.

The U.S. economy is improving. The rate of increase in employment has decreased. This coupled with the decrease and the rate of increase of inventory liquidation suggests an increase with an already evident increase of former commitments, which in turn suggests a general slowdown of the downturn of the slightly perceptible upturn of the downturn analysis which is about to occur. If you are concerned about the low level of economic indicators today, you should be. But remember that an upturn only occurs at the bottom of a downturn. . . .

A recent article in *U.S. News and World Report* (1978) poked fun at government bureaucratese and is worth mentioning.

Translating Bureaucratese

Government reforms come and go, but the language of public officials remains impenetrable. Some examples from official statements:

Interior Department: "Directly impact the visual quality of the present environment."

Translation: Spoil the view.

Food and Drug Administration: "Innovation processes should be considered to better integrate informed societal judgements and values into the regulatory mechanism."

Translation: Think.

Census Bureau: "Data users who make inferences about the nature of relationships between unrelated adults of the opposite sex who share the same living quarters are cautioned that the data shown here on this subject are aggregates which are distributed over a spectrum of categories including partners, resident employees, and roomers."

Translation: Couples who live together don't always sleep together.

The central idea should be clearly stated in the first paragraph Every good journalist provides the what, who, why, where, when, and how in the lead paragraph or as quickly as possible. Secretary Baldridge of the Commerce Department, in his speeches and memos to Commerce employees, emphasized the importance of clarity and brevity in effective written communication. The following is an actual memo distributed at a presentation made by Secretary Baldridge:

Clarity and brevity are key factors when preparing a letter to the secretary or deputy secretary. Secretary Baldridge wants short sentences and short words, with emphasis on plain English. Use no more words than effective expression requires.

Here are some guidelines:

• Answer questions specifically.

• The response should be no more than one page, where possible. When answering a series of questions, prepare a brief cover letter and attach specific answers.

- If the response is negative, be polite, not abrupt.

- Avoid wordiness. Keep sentences lean and short.

- Use the active rather than the passive voice.

- Use no unnecessary adjectives or adverbs. Write with nouns and verbs to strengthen letter.

- Do not use nouns or adjectives or adverbs. Write with nouns and verbs to strengthen letter.

- Do not use nouns or adjectives as verbs, such as:

to optimize	to finalize
to impact (or to impact on)	to target
to interfact	targeted
to maximize	

- Use the precise word or phrase.

  data (singular); *data* (plural)
  criterion (singular); criteria (plural)
  subsequent means after, not before
  different from, not different than
  insure means to guarantee against financial loss
  ensure means to make sure or certain
  effect as a noun means a result; as a verb, to bring about, to accomplish
  affect means to influence, to act upon, to alter, to assume, to adopt
  think is mental; feel is physical or emotional
  (think thoughts; feel feelings)

- Stop using affected or imprecise words. Some examples:

  viable
  input
  orient
  hopeful (use I hope)
  ongoing (prefer continuing)
  responsive
  specificity
  utilize (prefer use)
  glad (use pleased or happy)
  thrust
  effectuated
  output
  prioritize (not a verb)
  hereinafter
  parameter (use boundary or limit)

image
delighted
inappropriate (overused)

- Avoid redundancies, such as:

serious crisis
personally reviewed
new initiatives
enclosed herewith
important essentials
final outcome
future plans
end result
great majority
untimely death (Has there ever been a timely death?)

- Stop using the following phrases:

I share your concern (or *interest* or views)
I appreciate your concern (or interest or views)
I would hope (use I hope)
I regret I cannot be more responsive (or encouraging)
I am deeply concerned
Thank you for your letter expressing concern (use Thank you for your letter concerning)
prior to (use before)
subject matter
very much
bottom line
best wishes
at the present time (use now)
as you know, as I am sure you know, as you are aware
more importantly (use more important)
needless to say
it is my intention
mutually beneficial
contingent upon
management regime

- Do not use a split infinitive (such as placing an adverb between *to* and the verb)

- Do not use addressee's first name in the body of the letter

- Do not refer to the date of the incoming letter

- Stop apologizing, such as, "I regret the delay in responding to you."

As Secretary Baldridge says, "In short, halfway between Ernest Hemingway and Zane Grey, with no bureaucratese."

INFORMAL COMMUNICATION

Think back for a moment about information you have received via the grapevine, things like who's going into the Senior Executive Service, and who's getting incentive awards, what effect the merit pay system is going to have on your job, etc. It's very likely that much of the information you receive in your agency is via the grapevine—the informal pattern of communication that operates in every complex organization. It is useful for you to know about the general characteristics of grapevine activity and to have some techniques for coping with it in your own organization. Let's look at what is known about the grapevine:

The grapevine is fast   There are generally few restrictions on the grapevine because it is usually transmitted personally and doesn't follow any chain of command. Davis (1972) and Walton (1961), two researchers in grapevine activity, suggest it is one of the speediest channels for spreading information in organizations.

The grapevine is accurate   Davis (1967) has argued that in normal business situations, between 75 and 95 percent of grapevine information is correct, even though most stories are somewhat incomplete in their details. Other research appears to support these findings.

Grapevine information, like grapes, usually comes in bunches.   It is sometimes assumed that grapevine information travels in a straight line from person A to B to C, etc. Davis (1967) suggests differently:

> Many a "last to know" executive grumbles about the grapevine because he is under the impression that it operates like a long chain in which A tells B, who tells C, who then tells D, and so on until 20 persons later, T gets the information—very late and very incorrect. Not so. Some grapevines may operate that way, but research shows that they generally follow a different pattern, which works something like this:
>   A tells three or four others (such as B, R, and F). Yet only one or two of these receivers will then pass on the information, and they will usually tell more then pass on the information, and they will usually tell more than one person. Then, as the information becomes older and the proportion of those knowing it gets larger, it gradually dies out because those who receive it do not repeat it.

The grapevine versus rumor   Grapevine information and rumors are not really the same types of communication, even though they seem alike superficially. Rumors are usually unfounded, unsubstantiated bits of information. They can be very troublesome and can cause real problems for management. Ideally, rumors should be stopped as soon as possible because they can distort employees' perception about future events.

What can a manager do about the grapevine and rumors? Well, the first thing to remember is that you can't stop them from occurring. They are as inevitable as rain. You can, however, learn ways to control both rumors and the grapevine:

> Once a rumor has begun, make sure those who are most affected by it are given the accurate, most timely information.
>
> Use effective, consistent communication channels (i.e., those known to transmit information accurately and reliably) to convey accurate, timely information.
>
> Identify your *local influentials* (those employees who have high credibility among their peers) and make sure they have the accurate information.
>
> Construct or reconstruct messages so they are easily repeated verbatim.

An extremely interesting example of these principles occurred a few years ago at NASA's Space Flight Center at Huntsville, Alabama. When rumors were flying concerning Congressional budget cuts in the space program, Wernher Von Braun, a highly credible source, used closed circuit television to convey to all employees a consistent, accurate, and timely message on the status of the budget considerations. This procedure dealt with the rumors directly and curtailed future (and potentially inaccurate) perceptions of job security at NASA.

FORMAL CHANNELS OF COMMUNICATION

Formal communication channels emanate from sources that are considered official and therefore, have a sense of *legitimacy* about them. Formal channels move in three basic directions; downward, upward, and horizontally.

Downward Communication

Downward communication refers to those messages that flow vertically from supervisors to subordinates. There are essentially seven different types of downward communication:

1. Task instructions, "Type letters to senators and congressmen first";

2. Task rationales, "We do it this way because it's cheaper";
3. Organizational policies, "No annual leave may be taken in the first nine months";
4. Position descriptions, "These are the duties of a clerk/typist: . . . ";
5. Performance feedback, "Jim, your report was clear, accurate, and timely";
6. Mission statement or organizational goals, "Our job in Public Affairs is to publicize the department's programs."
7. Technological or organizational change, "We are implementing a new information processing system . . . . "

Although downward communication has been extensively studied in organizations, significant problems still exist in this area, such as information overload/underload. How do you feel when you need important information and you can't get it? Frustrated? Angry? Usually, employees become quite frustrated when ambiguity surrounds an important situation. As managers, you have the problem of giving people information they need without overburdening them with extra, unnecessary information. Maintaining a balance is difficult.

Another potential problem surrounding downward communication is whether it is timely. Management not only jeopardizes its credibility with untimely information, but also creates a ripe climate for rumors.

In a series of studies across sixteen organizations, Goldhaber and his associates (1977) concluded that:

Most employees don't receive the information they need to do their jobs effectively.

The primary information needs are primarily about personal job-related matters and secondarily about organizational decision making.

The best sources of accuracy, timeliness, etc., are from the employees' immediate environment, such as the immediate supervisor and co-workers. The worst sources of information appear to be top management.

Information from top management is considered to be of lower quality than that from other sources.

A more recent study conducted by the International Association of Business Communicators surveyed 45,662 employees of forty organizations in the United States and Canada, and found essentially the same results. Of consistent importance in these findings is the quality and amount of performance feedback given to employees. In a recent study I conducted, I asked a cross section of employees, "How do you know when you are doing a good job?" Their answers essentially were "No news is good news." Many respondents said that as long as they didn't hear anything from their supervisors, they assumed they were doing okay, because the only feedback they usually received was negative. But they quickly added that they didn't like the situation because they didn't know "where they stood" with their supervisors.

Upward Communication

Upward communication is concerned with messages that flow up the organization from subordinates to supervisor. Historically, management has placed little emphasis on upward communication. In my estimation, however, it is the most important type of communication with which management should be concerned. It provides managers with the feedback necessary to solve problems and make decisions; it also allows for employee involvement in the decision-making process.

Planty and Machaver (1952) say the value of effective upward communication is great because it:

> Helps management to understand its downward communication needs better
>
> Increases the likelihood that subordinates will accept decisions because they've had an opportunity to participate in the process
>
> Provides feedback about how well downward messages are understood and accepted
>
> Indicates how subordinates think and feel about their jobs, their associates, and their organization

What should be communicated upward? Planty and Machaver (1952) suggest the following things should be communicated upward in organizations:

> What subordinates are doing; highlights of their work; achievements; progress; and future job plans
>
> Outlines of unsolved work problems on which subordinates now need aid or may require help in the future
>
> Suggestions or ideas of subordinates for improvements within their department or in the company
>
> How subordinates think and feel about their jobs; their associates; and their organization

How can information be communicated upward? You may want to evaluate your present environment, and ask yourself how much emphasis is being placed on the importance of upward communication. Here are some areas in which you could encourage upward communication:

Staff meetings
Social gatherings
Lunch
Subordinates who are perceived as highly credible sources
Union publications
In-house publications
Employee grievances
Suggestion systems
Counseling sessions
Performance evaluation sessions
Career counseling sessions
Voluntary discussion sessions
Employee surveys

Upward communication is indispensable in the management of people. It provides information for effective planning, problem solving, and decision making, and also increases employee motivation, because it allows for employees to have more influence over their work environment. All of the above are dependent on one thing, however. It's your willingness to listen sensitively to what your employees have to say.

Horizontal Communication

Horizontal communication is concerned with the lateral flow of information throughout the organization, particularly (but not exclusively) across department, or division lines. Among the major barriers to horizontal communication are the different values, perceptions, assumptions, language, and loyalties held by people in different parts of the organization. For example, how often in your own experiences have there been communication problems between line and staff personnel; between research and development and operations; between engineers and accountants; or between personnel specialists and budget analysts?

Horizontal communication is extremely necessary for effective task coordination, information sharing, and problem solving. As organizations grow in size, the jobs become more specialized. While specialization is necessary, the effective organization also coordinates or integrates those specialized functions toward achieving the organization's mission.

In 1916 Henry Fayol realized the importance of horizontal communication when he proposed a "gang plank" to bridge separate authority lines one level below so two people with a single superior can have dialogue. Fayol's idea allowed subordinates in different functional units to communicate horizontally and directly with the permission of their supervisors, without breaking the chain of command. Effective managers respect the characteristics and importance of vertical and horizontal communication and take steps to see they are implemented properly.

COMMUNICATION CLIMATE

In preparing this book, I had the pleasure of interviewing a number of government officials. One particularly memorable interview was with an employee from the Department of Commerce. He provided some helpful insights about the future direction of government service and its communication requirements:

> The present Administration came in to make a major, fundamental change in the federal government. This change in and of itself creates disruption and anxiety, and the magnitude of the changes have created significant disruption. . . . We need to do the following things: (1) We need to teach our managers to treat people better; (2) We need to be able to rely on the integrity of others to keep their promises; (3) We need more face-to-face communication; (4) We need a more truthful and open communication climate; (5) We must set and communicate goals throughout the organization; (6) Subordinate goals must be participatory. . . . The most important factor of the future is how we will manage people in a climate of limited resources and changing values.

The last sentence above suggests a major challenge to all managers in the public sector. The pressure to cut federal spending is affecting all of us. What are the changing values of the American work force? Mindell and Gorden (1981) found that the contemporary American work force generally possessed the following values:

- Low loyalty or commitment to the organization
- A need for organizational recognition for contributions
- A need for rewards geared to motivate accomplishment
- Decreasing concern for job security and stability
- A view of leisure as being more important than work
- A need to perform work that is challenging and worthwhile
- A need to participate in decisions that affect them
- Stronger identification with a personal role than with a work role
- A need for communication from management about what's going on in the organization
- A need to rise above the routine, and approach tasks creatively
- A need for personal growth opportunities on the job

It's apparent from the above list that the contemporary employee chiefly wants a communication climate that fosters achievement and its recognition and the opportunity to influence decision making.

A few years ago I developed an instrument to measure the communication climates of organizations (Falcione 1978), which you and your employees can use in your own organizations. The instrument contains twenty-six items representing five factors of communication climate.

These factors are:

Factor 1 (eleven items)   Communication Receptivity
Factor 2 (four items)   Decision Making
Factor 3 (four items)   Organizational Commitment
Factor 4 (three items)   Coordination
Factor 5 (four items)   Communication Satisfaction

Communication Climate Inventory

For each item, you are to circle the number which reflects the *extent to which you agree* with the statement on the following five-point scale

1   to a very little extent
2   to a little extent
3   to some extent
4   to a great extent
5   to a very great extent

Communication Receptivity (Factor 1)

1. I feel free to bring up important things about the job with my supervisor.

    1   2   3   4   5

2. I feel free to talk over personal problems with my supervisor.

    1   2   3   4   5

3. If I disagree with a decision made by my supervisor, I would feel free to question his/her decision.

    1   2   3   4   5

4. I often have the opportunity to give additional ideas or information to my supervisor over and above what he/she's asked for.

    1   2   3   4   5

5. My ideas are given fair consideration by my supervisor.

    1   2   3   4   5

6. I get prompt answers to questions and suggestions sent to my supervisor.

    1   2   3   4   5

7. My supervisor is there when I need him/her.

    1   2   3   4   5

8. My supervisor lives up to his/her promises to me.

           1   2   3   4   5

9. My supervisor is aware of my work needs.

           1   2   3   4   5

10. My supervisor is aware of my abilities on the job.

           1   2   3   4   5

11. My supervisor has a sincere interest in my welfare.

           1   2   3   4   5

Decision Making (Factor 2)

1. My supervisor lets me make decisions.

           1   2   3   4   5

2. My supervisor asks for my opinion before he/she makes a decision which affects me.

           1   2   3   4   5

3. My supervisor asks for my opinion concerning decisions already made.

           1   2   3   4   5

4. Decisions made by my supervisor may be modified or changed after asking my opinion.

           1   2   3   4   5

Organizational Commitment (Factor 3)

1. This organization is sincerely interested in the welfare of its people.

           1   2   3   4   5

2. I have confidence in the honesty of this organization.

           1   2   3   4   5

3. This organization treats its members fairly.

           1   2   3   4   5

4. If I were starting over, I would want to work for this organization.

           1   2   3   4   5

Coordination (Factor 4)

1. People in this organization avoid creating problems or interference with each other's work duties and responsibilities.

           1   2   3   4   5

2. The coordination of the work in this organization is handled well.

           1   2   3   4   5

3. Work assignments are well planned in this organization.

           1   2   3   4   5

Communication Satisfaction (Factor 5)

1. This organization keeps me informed about what's going on in general.

           1   2   3   4   5

2. Policies and procedures are explained thoroughly to me.

    1   2   3   4   5

3. I know what is expected of me on the job.

    1   2   3   4   5

4. I am usually told in advance about forthcoming changes in personnel policies and procedures that affect my job.

    1   2   3   4   5

Add the numbers circled in each section. The total range of possible scores is from 26 (very poor communication climate) to 130 (very good communication climate).

Each factor can also be scored individually. The ranges per section are:

Factor 1   Communication Receptivity   11–55
Factor 2   Decision Making   4–20
Factor 3   Organizational Commitment   4–20
Factor 4   Coordination   3–15
Factor 5   Communication Satisfaction   4–20

After you've completed your score, go back to those items in which you marked 1 or 2 and place a check mark next to the items. This will give you a better idea of the specific areas that need improvement. Maintaining a healthy communication climate is critical to effective management.

OTHER FACTORS INFLUENCING COMMUNICATION CLIMATE

All organizations need to be particularly concerned with their goals and objectives if they want to thrive. Goals and objectives can be viewed on two levels: the organizational level and the individual level. I'd like to suggest two communication techniques that can help you and your employees achieve your goals and objectives more efficiently and effectively. The first is called the *Information Processing Meeting*; it deals with the organizational level. The second method is called the *Expectation Review*; it deals with the individual level.

Information Processing Meeting

Let's assume your particular agency, branch, division, unit, etc., has a set of opportunities or problems it needs to confront. This procedure can be done in one full day or can be broken down into individual steps if there are constraints. The following steps can be taken:

Step 1 The top manager of the group sets the climate by emphasizing the importance of what the group is about to do and what the goals of the session are: to confront problems or opportunities in an open manner, and to develop action plans for their resolution.

Step 2 Heterogenous groups are formed, with individuals from different functional units forming each group. Their task is to brainstorm the following questions:
a. What are the goals and objectives of this organization?
b. What are the critical issues or problems faced by this organization?
c. What are the external demands on this organization?

Step 3 Each group presents its list to the entire group. A facilitator synthesizes all lists and reproduces them for the entire group.

Step 4 Heterogenous groups now brainstorm the following questions:
a. What changes should be made in this organization?
b. If things could be different, how would they be? (Topic areas such as organizational structure, goals, relationships, management style, procedures, performance, formal/informal policies, can be given to expedite the process).

Step 5 Each group presents its list to the entire group. A facilitator synthesizes all lists and reproduces them for the entire group.

Step 6 Functional groups (those people who normally work together) are formed. Their task is to choose the top five change areas relevant to their functional group and rank them according to priority.

Step 7 Each functional group is to develop an Action Plan that is *specific* and *realistic*. Each plan must contain the following:
a. Objectives
b. Responsibilities (who, what, when, how)
c. Timetable
d. Criteria: how will you know that you've accomplished your objective?

Step 8 Each functional group presents its action plan to the entire group allowing for question and answers. After all plans have been presented, they are reproduced by the facilitator and disseminated later to all functional groups.

Step 9 The top manager reconvenes the entire group to reinforce the commitment to achieving the goal set forth in the action plans, but still reserves the right to modify individual plans where necessary.

Step 10   Entire group reconvenes after a set period of time to report on progress of action plans.

I have used this procedure on a number of occasions and have found it an efficient technique for both goal setting and action planning.

The Expectation Review Technique

For a moment, think about any problem you may have had or are having with someone. No matter what the specific content of the problem was or is, my guess is that it can be reduced to a very basic conflict. At one point or another there was a *violation of expectations*. In all interpersonal relationships, sets of expectations are developed about how the other person should behave or perform. When they are violated, uncertainty usually follows, then anxiety about the uncertainty sets in. As supervisors, we need to have fairly continuous, ongoing feedback with our subordinates to minimize the violation of expectations. Whenever you make decisions or take an action that will affect your subordinate, and you don't discuss that action or decision, you create the potential for expectations to be violated. You are acting *independently* in a relationship which needs to be *interdependent* if it is to prosper.

Another factor adds to the complexity of the situation. Remember, we judge ourselves on the basis of our *intentions* but others judge us on the basis of our *behavior*. They don't know what our intentions are. Because the criteria by which we judge ourselves and others differ, the violation of expectations becomes much more probable. If a supervisor/subordinate relationship is to grow and achieve both individual and organizational goals, there must be a periodic renegotiation of expectations. This can be done systematically by implementing the *Expectation Review Process* (Chicota and Falcione 1980). Simply put, the procedure is a formalized program in which the manager and the employee sit together and list the expectations each has of the other. These lists are discussed mutually every three months, and disparities concerning functions, performance, goals, and future opportunities are renegotiated where necessary. This prevents surprises in the annual performance appraisal (discussed in more detail in Chapter 3) because the manager and the employees have maintained a structured dialogue throughout the performance period. The following model exemplifies the process.

How you decide to set up the Expectation Review is up to you. The criteria you and your subordinate decide to discuss will be a function of your specific job. The important ingredients, however, are that the process is structured, with time mutually set aside, and criteria mutually agreed upon, with both parties being clear on what their expectations are in the process.

The techniques described thus far can help increase your effective-

FIGURE 2.1   Expectation Review Process

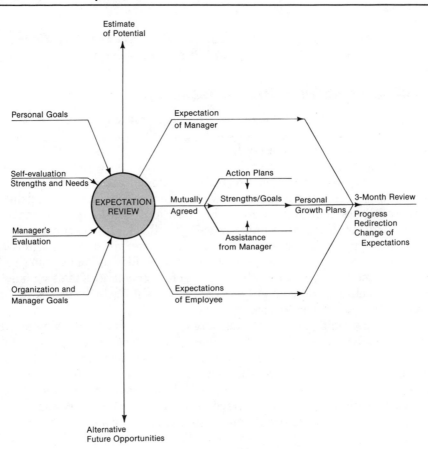

ness as a manager, but the one factor that makes the difference between successful and unsuccessful managers is *credibility*. Let's take a look at what constitutes supervisor credibility and how you can construct your own and your boss's credibility profile. Then I will offer suggestions on how you can enhance your credibility on the job.

Perceived Supervisor Credibility

The quality of the supervisor/subordinate relationship can be a significant contributor to job satisfaction and productivity. If there is a lack of trust in the relationship, research indicates information is distorted and concealed by employees. One of the major contingencies affecting how much subordinates trust their managers is their perception of the manager's credibility. There are a number of perceived credibility factors that contribute in one degree or another to the subordinate's satisfaction.

My own research (Falcione 1974) shows there are four credibility factors that affect employee satisfaction:

1. Safety—How safe do I feel about my manager's honesty, sociability, character, etc.?
2. Competence—Is my manager experienced, informed, well trained?
3. Extroversion—Is my manager assertive, active, etc.?
4. Emotional stability—Does my manager remain calm; poised under stressful situations?

In my estimation, perceived credibility is the most significant variable in effective superior/subordinate transactions. If a manager is perceived as lacking in credibility, his or her effectiveness is limited dramatically. If employees view the manager as having low credibility, they won't be able to trust his or her decisions or intentions, and the viability of the relationship diminishes.

Credibility Profile

If you'd like to measure your own credibility profile or that of your own boss, complete the following scale.

Each item has a seven point scale. The low end (1) indicates low credibility on that item; the high end (7) indicates high credibility. Think of a specific person (your manager or supervisor) and complete the scale. The scale's possible range for all items is 30 (very low credibility) to 210 (very high credibility). The range for Safety is 14–98; for Competence, 5–35; for Extroversion, 7–49; and for Emotional stability, 4–28.

Dimension		Scales	
Safety	dishonest	1 2 3 4 5 6 7	honest
Sociability	unfriendly	1 2 3 4 5 6 7	friendly
	unpleasant	1 2 3 4 5 6 7	pleasant
	awful	1 2 3 4 5 6 7	nice
	irritable	1 2 3 4 5 6 7	good-natured
	dangerous	1 2 3 4 5 6 7	safe
	negativistic	1 2 3 4 5 6 7	cooperative
	unjust	1 2 3 4 5 6 7	just
	selfish	1 2 3 4 5 6 7	unselfish
	unfair	1 2 3 4 5 6 7	fair
	unethical	1 2 3 4 5 6 7	ethical
	headstrong	1 2 3 4 5 6 7	mild
	sinful	1 2 3 4 5 6 7	virtuous
	jealous	1 2 3 4 5 6 7	not jealous

Competence	untrained	1 2 3 4 5 6 7	trained
Expertise	inexperienced	1 2 3 4 5 6 7	experienced
	uninformed	1 2 3 4 5 6 7	informed
	inexpert	1 2 3 4 5 6 7	expert
	unskilled	1 2 3 4 5 6 7	skilled
Extroversion	slow	1 2 3 4 5 6 7	fast
Dynamism	timid	1 2 3 4 5 6 7	bold
	meek	1 2 3 4 5 6 7	aggressive
	hesitant	1 2 3 4 5 6 7	emphatic
	cautious	1 2 3 4 5 6 7	adventurous
	forceless	1 2 3 4 5 6 7	forceful
	passive	1 2 3 4 5 6 7	active
Emotional stability	nervous	1 2 3 4 5 6 7	poised
Temperament	anxious	1 2 3 4 5 6 7	calm
	excitable	1 2 3 4 5 6 7	composed
	tense	1 2 3 4 5 6 7	poised

IMPROVING YOUR CREDIBILITY

Now that you have a better idea of what credibility is and how to measure it, I'd like to ask you to evaluate your own behavior and suggest ways to enhance your credibility with your subordinates.

The following checklist may give you some insight into your own behavior on the job. Place a check-mark next to the behavior you find yourself doing on the job.

_____ Failing to keep promises

_____ Failing to do your part on a mutual project

_____ Being late—missing deadlines

_____ Ignoring policies

_____ Releasing confidential information

_____ Making excessive errors or mistakes

_____ Giving the wrong information

_____ Losing files or records

_____ Spreading rumors instead of stopping them

_____ Circumventing normal communication channels

_____ Being unreceptive to employee concerns

_____ Being an ineffective listener

_____ Blaming others for your mistakes

_____ Appearing arbitrary in your decision making

_____ Failing to provide a rationale for decisions

How many did you check? Were you honest with yourself? If you want to enhance your credibility, I suggest that you work at behaviors that will enable you to erase the checkmarks in the above list. Your credibility, as perceived by others, is your most important asset in effective supervision. It is easy to lose, but very difficult to regain!

MOTIVATION IN GOVERNMENT ORGANIZATIONS

If the average government manager were asked to give advice about motivating others, what would he or she say? Very often the advice would range from, "You need to talk to your employees more," to, "Employees' jobs need to be more enriching." Both are somewhat ambiguous statements. It's interesting that, in my experience as a consultant to government agencies, I have found many managers able to talk about various theories of motivation, but few who were able to describe specific communication behaviors that relate to motivation. It really doesn't matter how many motivation theories you are familiar with, if you can't communicate effectively. Remember what I said in Chapter 1: We judge ourselves on the basis of our intentions (we intend to motivate effectively), while others judge us on the basis of our behaviors. Let's take a brief look at some of the motivation theories, and then identify what communication behaviors are needed.

Need Satisfaction Theory

As a practicing manager, you've probably heard Abraham Maslow's (1954) hierarchy of needs discussed in many management training courses. To refresh your memory, the hierarchy is reproduced here:

5 Self-Realization, Competence, and Achievement

4 Self-Esteem/Ego Status Needs

3 Social/Belongingness Needs

2 Security/Safety Needs

1 Physiological Needs

Recent research (Lawler 1976) suggests that an additional human need is just as important, particularly within the work environment. It is the need for self-control and independence. Unionization in the United States has concentrated on satisfying the first two basic needs, by providing fringe benefits. But the interesting thing about fringe benefits is that they often can only be used outside the work environment. Historically, at least, neither unions nor management have concentrated on satisfying the other human needs within the work environment. It also should be noted that the first four needs on the list can be satisfied by external means while the need for self-realization is more readily satisfied internally, by the person's own feelings of accomplishment and growth. Some recent additional research conclusions about human needs (Lawler and Rhode 1976) are worth noting:

1. Needs are arranged in a two level hierarchy. At the lower level are existence and security needs. At the higher level are social, esteem, autonomy, and self-realization needs.

2. The higher level needs will appear only when the lower level needs are satisfied.

3. Most needs can only be satisfied by extrinsic outcomes but the highest level needs can only be satisfied by intrinsic outcomes.

4. All needs except self-realization can be satisfied, and as they become satisfied, they become less important. Self-realization needs appear to be insatiable.

5. A person can be motivated by more than one need at a given time and will continue to be motivated by these needs until they are satisfied or until satisfaction of lower needs is threatened.

Two-Factor Theory of Motivation

Nearly two decades ago, Fredrick Herzberg wrote *Work and the Nature of Man*, presenting his research on motivation. He found there are two factors: *hygiene factors* and *satisfiers*. The hygiene factors consist of imperatives experienced by workers, but which are not, in and of themselves, motivators; they are often, in fact, sources of dissatisfaction. These hygiene factors consist of environmental characteristics such as company policy and administration, supervision, work conditions, salary, job status, and security.

The satisfiers, on the other hand, consist of such things as a sense of achievement, recognition, the work itself, having responsibility, growth, and advancement. Herzberg feels that if managers concentrate on the hygiene factors to motivate people, they will probably keep workers from being highly dissatisfied, but they will not tend to motivate. Instead, the manager is more likely to hear a question like, "What have you done for me lately?" Herzberg concluded that while the hygiene factors are important, true motivation occurs when workers feel a sense of achievement from their work, and are recognized for it. The following listings show the similarities between Maslow's Need Theory and Herzberg's Two-Factor Theory.

Maslow	*Herzberg*
Self-realization and fulfillment	Work itself
	Achievement
	Possibility of growth
	Responsibility
Esteem and status	Advancement
	Recognition
Belonging and social activity	Status
	Interpersonal relations
	Supervision
	Peers
	Subordinates
Safety and security	Supervision—Technical
	Company policy and administration
	Job security
Physiological needs	Working conditions
	Salary
	Personal life

A recent study was done at the Social Security Administration (SSA) to see if Herzberg's conclusions held true for government workers (Wasiniak 1980). The study used two questionnaires, one for first line supervisors and one for subordinates. Most of the questionnaire items were developed from five basic issues:

1. What motivates nonsupervisory employees to do a good job?
2. To what extent are first line supervisors aware of these motivations?
3. Are there any significant differences in employee motivators according to age, sex, or length of time on the job?
4. How much control do first line supervisors maintain over these motivators?
5. How much control do first line supervisors *think* they maintain over these motivators?

Table 2.1 contains the results of the study, from which the following conclusions can be drawn:

TABLE 2.1

Motivators	Rank	Percentage Selecting	Rank	Percentage Selecting	Percentage Difference
	Employees' Rating		Supervisors' Rating		Contrast
1. The ratings on your next performance appraisal	9	49	9	59	+10
2. Your possibility of an award	16	32	14	37	+ 5
3. Your personal work–related goals	4	83	5	72	−11
4. Good physical working conditions	15	34	15	33	− 1
5. Your feelings of loyalty and friendship for your supervisor	18	18	16	31	+13
6. Your opportunity to do interesting work	5	75	8	60	−15
7. The possibility of higher salary	88	51	13	41	−10
8. Your desire not to let your group down	13	38	10	53	+15
9. Recognition by your peers	12	40	2	79	+39
10. The possibility of promotion	6	71	4	73	+ 2
11. Feelings of achievement from doing challenging work well	1	96	6	69	−27
12. The possibility of disciplinary action by your supervisor	20	3	17	23	+20
13. Being part of a team	16	32	11	52	+20
14. Your inner need to always try to do a good job	2	94	7	68	−26
15. Strong job security	14	36	18	20	−16
16. Appreciation and recognition from your supervisor	10	42	2	79	+37
17. Your opportunity to do work you feel is important	3	88	1	81	− 7
18. Your desire to help the agency attain its goals	7	57	20	7	−50
19. The possibility of increased freedom on the job	11	41	12	48	+ 7
20. Being appointed the leader	19	10	19	11	+ 1

1. Out of twenty motivators, employees ranked achievement-oriented motivators highest, followed by recognition-oriented.
2. There appear to be no significant different in the top motivators of employees according to age, sex, and length of time in current positions.
3. First line supervisors, as a group, do not appear to have a

good grasp of factors which motivate employees. Achievement is underrated and recognition is overrated.

4. Supervisor perceptions of employees' desire to help the agency reach its goals are underrated.
5. Supervisors preceive employees to be more extrinsically than intrinsically motivated.
6. Supervisors appear to have significantly less control than they think they have over the strongest employee motivation.

How representative these conclusions are beyond SSA is difficult to say. You might think about how these conclusions might relate to your own agency.

CHARACTERISTICS THAT MOTIVATE

There are certain characteristics that contribute to whether a job motivates (Lawler and Rhode 1976).

1. The job should allow a worker to feel personally responsible for a meaningful portion of his or her work. Autonomy is of particular importance here.
2. The job must be meaningful and worthwhile to the individual. The worker should be able to identify with the task.
3. The job should be sufficiently whole pieces of work so that workers can perceive they have produced or accomplished something of significance.
4. The job should have a variety that challenges.
5. The job should provide feedback about what is accomplished, either from the job itself or from the supervisor.

LEADERSHIP IN GOVERNMENT ORGANIZATIONS

Now that we've taken a short look at motivation, it seems appropriate to conclude this chapter with a look at leadership. A manager will find it difficult to lead if he or she doesn't understand what motivates people, and one of the manager's tasks of leadership is to create an environment in which people feel motivated.

This kind of leadership is essential to good government. Every year in our local, state, and national elections, we hear the campaign slogans

TABLE 2.2 Styles of Leadership

Leadership Style	Leader Behavior	Efficiency	Morale
Informs	Manager makes decisions alone and then informs the group directly and clearly. Little interaction takes place.	Fast.	Short-term only; tends to create morale problems over long term.
Persuades	Manager decides what to do, but favors compromise and majority vote as means of persuading the group to accept the decisions. Manager usually determines who's for or against the decision *before* a group meeting takes place, and is prepared to discuss advantages and disadvantages.	Takes more time.	Tends to create morale problems over long term; tends to divide the group.
Consults	Manager makes the final decision, but only on the basis of input from the group; allows for the group's opinions to influence the final decision.	Takes considerable time.	Usually builds morale both in short and long term—as long as manager allows for opinions to have some degree of influence on the final decisions.
Participates	Manager shares the responsibility for decision making with the group. Manager questions, clarifies, summarizes periodically, but prefers the decision to be made by consensus.	Takes considerably more time to make decisions.	Usually builds morale both in short and long term; group has opportunity to contribute to problem solving and decision making; very conducive to high morale.

Probable Outcomes

Creativity	Complexity	Effectiveness	Control	Acceptance
Low.	Can't deal with highly complex problems because of information overload.	Long-term; poor.	Centralized in leader.	Usually poor, particularly over long term.
Better, but still limited by making decisions first.	Limited ability to deal with complexity; creates an atmosphere of winners and losers.	Long-term; tends to create an atmosphere of manipulation and distrust.	Manager loses some control; must rely on persuasive skills and influence strategies.	Long-term; poor; tends to create camps of winners and losers. Problem orientation becomes confirmed by who's for or against a decision.
Good; allows for many viewpoints to be heard.	Good; manager is in a better position to make the decision if he or she has all the information and views available.	Good both in short and long term.	Manager still maintains control over decision making; expectations between manager and subordinates are clear-cut.	Usually a high degree of acceptance as long as subordinates believe that they have been listened to, and that their opinions have some influence.
Very high; allows for all viewpoints to be expressed and discussed.	Very good because total group is free to express opinions and give information which will have some influence; the members tend to be more problem-oriented and can deal with complexity better because they have more information to work with.	Very high; decisions are usually better both in short and long terms.	Manager tends to lose some control over the group; must be more concerned about the group processes rather than station; not always so easy.	Very high because group is allowed to contribute in a meaningful way by participating, there tends to be higher commitment to those decisions which are made.

advocating the necessity for *new leadership*. That word is used so often in organizations that one might think of it as a simple construct. But it is far from that. Volumes have been written about leadership in the attempt to define it, and not surprisingly, approaches taken toward leadership have determined how it has been defined. The three main approaches consist of identifying leadership traits, leadership styles, and leadership contingencies. Let's take a look at each approach and see which might be most appropriate for you.

Trait Approach

Historically, leadership was explained as a set of traits based on the personality or the character of the leader, suggesting that all leaders possessed some inherent traits that made that effective. Little evidence was produced, however, to show that leaders had traits different from their followers. Leadership is more complex than a mere set of traits. It consists largely of the dynamics of the relationship developed among leaders and followers (managers and workers), and the perceptions of influence and status acquired from active participation.

Style Approach

The style approach to understanding leadership assumes that different styles have different effects on morale and productivity. The main styles of leadership can be summarized as *Informs, Persuades, Consults, and Participates*. Each of these styles is a pure form and may be more or less effective in different circumstances. In fact, the truly effective manager is one who is able to change styles to respond to each new situation. Tables 2.2 and 2.3 define the pure styles and show the potential consequence of each.

In summary, this chapter was designed to provide you with helpful suggestions for improving your written communication skills, and an opportunity to assess yourself as a manager. More specifically, you were given various tools which could be very helpful to you, as well as specific suggestions for creating a motivating environment through effective leadership and communication skills.

References

Chicta, M., & R. L. Falcione. August 1972. *The expectation review.* Unpublished working paper.

Davis, K. 1967. *Human relations at work.* New York: McGraw-Hill.

TABLE 2.3 Leadership Contingencies
When Should You Use the Different Styles?

Style	When to use it
Inform	Usually should be used in critical situations, such as an immediate deadline, when the manager doesn't have time for group participation. This style is also more appropriate when basic skills or instructions must be learned, when the subordinates don't have much experience or training in the job at hand, and for minor decisions, with no long-term consequences.
Persuade	Can be used in those instances when the manager feels inhibited in being open about an issue or problem. At times, a manager may feel impelled to withhold some information from the group. The dilemma, however, occurs when the group doesn't understand the total situation, and it becomes more difficult for the manager to identify the specific areas of resistance which need to be dealt with rhetorically. Generally, advisable to use when there is a directive from a higher level, and the group is asked to accept the order or be prepared to compromise. In order for the manager to implement the style successfully, he/she must be aware of all the advantages and disadvantages of acceptance and/or compromise. The manager must also be skilled in dealing rhetorically with their differences.
Consult	Can be used when the group is skilled and knowledgeable with experience in working together. The manager needs considerable time to implement this style effectively. Should be used when the decision will affect those in the group, and when the problem is large and complex. Do not use this style if you have already made the decision. If you do, you run the risk of blowing your credibility, and you don't want to do that.
Participate	Can be used when the group is very knowledgeable, skilled, informed, and experienced—if they are to be affected by the decision, and you need their commitment. Do not use this style if you are concerned about your own status and control and if you are not willing to go along with the consensus of the group. This approach is also very risky for the manager if he/she is seeking a compromise or if the decision had already been made prior to discussion.

Falcione, R. L. 1974. The factor structure of source credibility scales for immediate supervisors in the organizational context. *Central States Speech Journal*, 25:63–66.

Falcione, R. L. 1975. Subordinate satisfaction as a function of perceived supervisor credibility. Paper presented at a meeting of the International Communication Association, Chicago, Illinois.

Falcione, R. L., J. C. McCroskey, & J. A. Daly. 1977. Job satisfaction as a function of employees' communication apprehension, self-esteem, and perceptions of their immediate supervisors. Paper presented at a meeting of the International Communication Associations, Berlin, Germany.

Falcione, R. L. 1978. Subordinate satisfaction as a function of communication climate and perceptions of immediate supervision. Paper presented at the Eastern Communication Association Convention, Boston, Massachusetts.

Goldhaber, G., D. Porter, & M. Yates. The ICA communication audit survey instrument: 1977 organizational norms. Paper presented at meeting of the International Communication Association, Berlin, Germany.

Herzberg, Fredrick. 1966. *Work and the nature of man.* New York: World.

Lawler, E. E., & J. H. Rhode. 1976. *Information and control in organizations.* CA: Goodyear.

Maslow, A. 1954. *Motivation and personality.* New York: Harper & Row.

Mindell, M. G. & W. I. Gorden. 1981. Employees values in a changing society. AMA Management Briefing. AMACOM, New York.

Planty, E. & W. Machaver. 1952. Upward communications: A project in executive development. *Personnel,* 1952, 28-4, 304–378. In *Interpersonal and organizational communication,* edited by Richard C. Huseman, Cal M. Logue, and Dwight L. Freshley. Boston, Massachusetts: Holbrook Press, 1977.

U.S. News & World Report, October 26, 1978, 26.

Walton, E. 1961. How efficient is the grapevine? *Personnel:* 45–49.

Wasiniak, R. E. 1980. What really motivates workers? *Management.*

CHAPTER 3

Communication and Managing Others

MEMO

TO: Reader
FR: Author
RE: Chapter 3

This chapter examines the importance of communication skills when managing others, particularly when you must appraise and counsel employees. You'll be exploring the following topics:

1. Evaluating the performance of others
2. Basic performance appraisal program
3. Planning for the appraisal
4. Using descriptive language
5. Asking questions effectively
6. Active listening skills
7. Managing differences
8. Asserting yourself nondefensively
9. Coaching and counseling others
10. A Generic Communication Skills Model
11. Providing career guidance to others

Thus far, this book has emphasized the importance of effective communication in the management of people in government service. This chapter is designed to provide you with some specific skills which will help in making your managerial job easier and more effective. The skills emphasized include interpersonal level skills, such as the appropriate use of language, question techniques, active listening techniques, and resolving differences. A generic communication skills model will also be presented. This will help you particularly in coaching and counseling situations. The last area of skill development focuses on career counseling.

EVALUATING THE PERFORMANCE OF OTHERS

The objective of the 1978 Civil Service Reform Act (CSRA) was to improve the efficiency and effectiveness of the government by increasing management authority and employee protection. The major features of the Act are to provide for:

> An equitable appeals process
>
> Protection against merit pay abuses
>
> Incentives and rewards for good work and efficient, effective management

Let's look at the communication implications the CSRA has for you as a supervisor or manager. Beginning in 1981, the act provided an unprecedented system for tying pay increases for GS–13s through GS–15s directly to performance, rather than to time in grade or service. All employees under the system no longer receive automatic within grade increases; pay increases are now based on merit. What does this mean from a communication perspective? Since the act emphasizes the relationship between pay and performance, it gives particular importance to effective performance appraisals. Section 430 of the CSRA calls specifically for performance appraisals to be held with all federal employees. Each agency is responsible for developing its own appraisal system, with OPM approval.

Performance appraisals under the new system are vital to the effective working relationship between supervisors and subordinates. They form the basis for decisions to train, reward, counsel, assign, promote, demote, retain, or remove employees.

As members of the federal bureaucracy, I'm sure you've heard horror stories of the way performance appraisals have been conducted. Examples range from sliding the rating sheet across the desk and asking for it to be signed, to sending it via mail to be signed and returned. In contrast, the new system stresses, indeed requires, a dialogue between supervisor and subordinate, stressing employee participation and involvement in the process.

Employee involvement is specifically called for in developing performance standards, which are based on the critical elements of the job. The procedure by which the critical elements are developed must be recorded in writing before rather than after the formal appraisal. Thus, the employee's appraisal must be based on how well he or she performed the critical requirements of the job. It is important to note that the employee must be appraised on job performance alone, and cannot be compared to other employees. The appraisal must be conducted at least yearly and the conclusions drawn must be made in writing.

Specifically, the new appraisal systems designed for each agency must:

- Advise employees on what the critical elements of their job are
- Establish performance standards that permit an accurate evaluation of performance, based on objective, job-related criteria
- Reassign, demote, or remove those employees who continue to perform poorly—but only after an opportunity has been given to improve performance

The relationship between conducting effective performance appraisals and using effective communication skills is obvious. It does not matter how much you know about the performance appraisal system in your agency, if you can't communicate that system well, then it doesn't matter how viable the system is. It just won't work for you!

The Civil Service Reform Act (CSRA) requires that all federal agencies develop one or more performance appraisal systems, using performance elements and performance standards. Before we consider the specific communication skills necessary in an effective performance appraisal, it would be useful to define the basic characteristics of an appraisal program. The following definitions come from the Department of the Navy, and are representative of other federal agencies:

BASIC PERFORMANCE APPRAISAL PROGRAM

1. Definitions
   a. *Performance appraisal system*   A system which identifies performance elements and critical performance elements, establishes performance standards, communicates standards and elements to employees, establishes performance appraisal methods and procedures, and provides for the appropriate use of appraisal information in making personnel decisions.
   b. *Performance*   The accomplishment of assigned duties and responsibilities by an employee.
   c. *Performance element*   Any major component (i.e., duty, task, requirement, responsibility, or objective) of a position, for which the employee is held accountable, and performance of which contributes meaningfully to the success or failure in performing the duties of that position.

    d. *Critical performance element* A performance element of sufficient importance to a position that performance below the satisfactory performance standard established by management would require remedial action and denial of a within-grade increase. Unsatisfactory performance on a critical performance element may be the basis for removing or reducing the grade level of that employee. Such action may be taken without regard to performance on other components of the job.

    e. *Performance standards* The expressed measure of the level of achievement established by management for the performance elements of a position or groups of positions. Measurement factors may include, but are not limited to, elements such as quantity, quality, and timeliness.

2. Level of Performance

    a. Standards will be described in writing for at least the highly satisfactory and marginal performance levels for each critical performance element established. When noncritical performance elements are used as a part of the appraisal process, both the noncritical performance element and the standard for the highly satisfactory and marginal performance levels must also be recorded in writing.

    Supervisors must rate performance, in writing, on each critical performance element and each noncritical element, if established, in one of the following five levels:

    U Unsatisfactory Performance which fails to meet the marginal performance standard and is unacceptable. Usually the employee's performance will show serious deficiencies in terms of quantity, quality, or timeliness.

    M Marginal Performance which meets the marginal performance standard; improvement is needed.

    S Satisfactory Performance which falls between the marginal and highly satisfactory standards; all requirements are met.

    H Highly Satisfactory Performance meets the highly satisfactory standard; requirements more than fully met.

    O Outstanding Performance significantly exceeds the highly satisfactory standard and is truly exceptional.

    b. An employee's cumulative performance on noncritical performance elements may decrease a summary performance rating of satisfactory, highly satisfactory or outstanding by no more than one performance level or increase a summary rating of satisfactory by no more than one level. However, performance on noncritical performance elements cannot be used to alter a summary performance rating of marginal or unsatisfactory. Accordingly, supervisors will use the following criteria to assign an overall performance rating which best describes the employee's overall performance:

U   Unsatisfactory—This rating will be assigned when any critical element has been rated *U* and indicates that performance in the job is unacceptable. Corrective action must be taken.

M   Marginal—This rating will be assigned if any critical element has been rated *M* and indicates that improvement in performance is needed.

S   Satisfactory—All critical elements are rated *S* or better and overall performance is generally described as satisfactory.

H   Highly Satisfactory—All critical elements are rated *S* or better, most are rated *H* or better, and overall performance is clearly better than satisfactory.

O   Outstanding—Performance is rated *O* on all critical performance elements for which standards have been established. Performance significantly exceeds satisfactory and is truly exceptional. A written justification is required to show how performance on critical performance elements was truly exceptional.

The performance appraisal form shown in Figure 3.1 has been used by government agencies and provides us with a good example, even though the form may vary from agency to agency.

Figures 3.2 and 3.3 show the pre-appraisal cycle activity which develops critical elements and performance standards, and the actual performance cycle recommended in the Civil Service Reform Act.

Now that we have a basic performance appraisal system in mind, we can look at the key communication skills necessary for the system to work effectively. In order for the performance appraisal to be mutually beneficial, managers need to be concerned with the following skills: (1) planning for the appraisal, (2) using descriptive language when evaluating performance, (3) asking questions effectively, and (4) listening actively to the employee.

PLANNING FOR THE APPRAISAL

In planning for the appraisal, you should look over the written and previously agreed upon performance standards, performance elements,

FIGURE 3.1 Performance Appraisal Form

EMPLOYEE'S NAME	Last	First	Middle Initial	OFFICIAL POSITION TITLE/SERIES/GRADE	
ORGANIZATION UNIT (Division, Branch, etc.)			Org. Code	OFFICIAL DUTY STATION	Address or Duty Station
Column A PERFORMANCE ELEMENT (List performance elements below. Designate critical elements by entering C in the bracket below the element number.)	Column B PERFORMANCE STANDARDS (Indicate level, i.e., marginal, highly satisfactory, etc.)		Column C PROGRESS REVIEW RESULTS, COMMENTS ASSUMPTION/CONDITIONS, O JUSTIFICATION		Column D RATING
1. [ ]					
2. [ ]					
3. [ ]					
4. [ ]					

5. [ ]

6. [ ]

7. [ ]

Summary Rating

RATING PERIOD: From: _____ To: _____

CERTIFICATION

Signature indicates that a particular step has been completed and understood by all parties.
(Date your signature)

APPRAISAL STAGES	EMPLOYEE		SUPERVISOR		REVIEWER	
Elements/Standards Set	Signature	Date	Signature	Date	Signature	Date
Progress Review(s)	Signature	Date	Signature	Date	Signature	Date
	Signature	Date	Signature	Date	Signature	Date
Annual Performance Appraisal	Signature	Date	Signature	Date	Signature	Date

FIGURE 3.2   *Performance Appraisal Program*

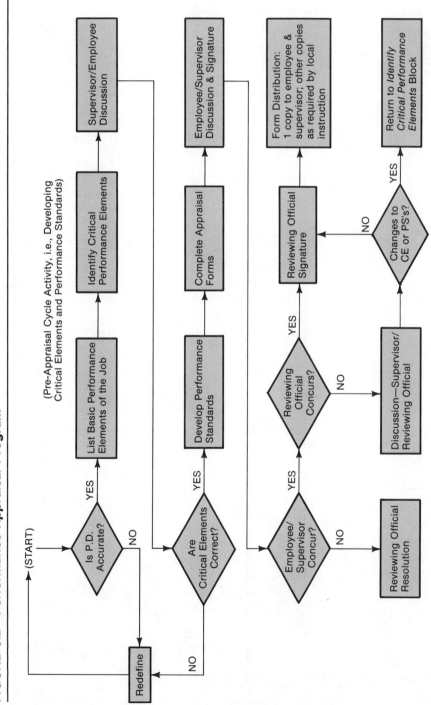

and critical performance elements of the employee's job. Have written behavioral documentation of employee's performance, making sure you have examples of particularly effective or ineffective performance. Keeping records is particularly important because it allows you to be more precise in your feedback and minimizes the likelihood of recent performance (good or bad) unduly influencing the evaluation. The employee should be informed about the upcoming appraisal and what will be appraised. He or she should also be informed of the date of the appraisal, and asked to think about his or her performance since the last appraisal, giving particular thought to critical elements of the job and problems encountered, as well as his or her own achievements.

Your opening remarks should also be considered in the planning process. It is sometimes suggested that the manager should start the appraisal with small talk to put the employee at ease and develop rapport. This can be an ineffective way of opening the session, especially if the employee perceives a lack a genuineness. The opening should include a statement of purpose, an overview of the process, your expectation of what can be gained from the appraisal, an expression of the importance of candor and mutual dialogue so that you both can grow from the experience. Effective planning prior to the session and at the opening can set the proper climate for a mutually productive appraisal.

USING DESCRIPTIVE LANGUAGE

After you have sufficiently planned for the appraisal and opened the session positively, you must now give feedback to the employee on his or her performance. The particular skill to use here is extremely important. You must describe performance behaviors objectively rather than evaluate the employee's performance on inferential criteria. Evaluative comments are the primary barriers to effective communication because they tend to create defensive reactions in others. Further, defensive behavior usually engenders defensive behavior in others, and the barrier building escalates; we tend to stop listening to one another.

Look at the list below and place an E next to the words or phrases that are evaluative and a D next to words or phrases that are descriptive.

1. "Jack has a good attitude."
2. "Alice is extremely diligent."
3. "Peter missed three deadlines."
4. "You ought to be cooperative, like Phil."
5. "No one shows as much initiative as Bill."

FIGURE 3.3 *Performance Appraisal: A Management Tool*

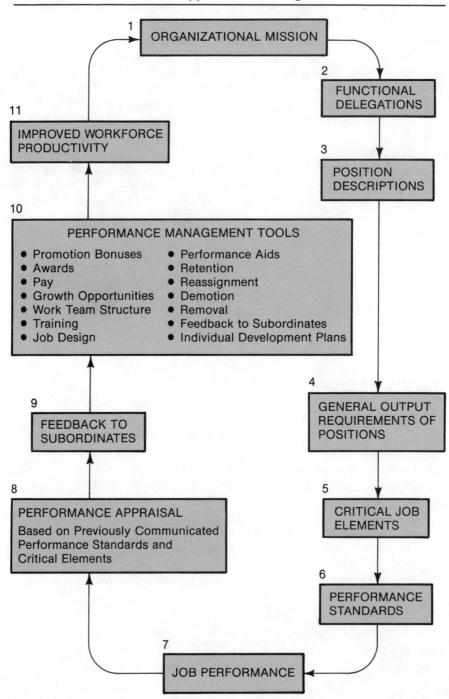

6. "The group manager commented that Joan presents work papers on time."
7. "Rita never takes work home."
8. "Art, that was very unprofessional of you."

Obviously, 1, 2, 4, 5, and 8 are all evaluative phrases. They don't provide very specific, descriptive information of behavior. If you use evaluative phrases when giving performance feedback, you will, in all likelihood, create some communication problems for yourself.

Sandra O'Connell (1979) has done an excellent job of explaining the characteristics of language that is purely descriptive. Descriptive language:

Tells about events or behavior
Can be observed and verified by others
Is specific and concrete
Uses action verbs
Is qualified rather than absolute
Is relatively free of value judgment
Does not attribute motives
Is more likely to gain agreement

Take a look at the columns below. If you were on the receiving end, which would you prefer?

Description of Behavior	*Evaluation of Behavior*
When you arrive late for work six times in two weeks	When you ignore the agency
When you don't follow each phase in the standard operating procedure	When you do sloppy work
When you left the meeting	When you got bored and left early

Let's take a minute to practice writing descriptive statements. The following statements are obviously evaluative in nature. Rewrite each statement, making it descriptive. Use your own work environment as a frame of reference.

1. You need to be more cooperative in meetings.

    Alternative:_____

2. You did a great job on the project! Keep it up!

    Alternative:_____

3. You're just not a team player . . .

   Alternative:_____

4. I've rated you low in initiative because I feel you have a poor attitude.

   Alternative:_____

5. You never find enough time to get all the work finished.

   Alternative:_____

6. Jim, you're not very professional.

   Alternative:_____

It should be noted that individuals need specific, descriptive feedback on their performance even when the feedback is positive. Telling an employee that a good job was performed is fine, but it's also important to convey what was good about it so the employee can continue to perform according to your expectations and grow. It is imperative to be specific and descriptive when giving positive or negative performance feedback.

ASKING QUESTIONS EFFECTIVELY

How often have you conducted a performance appraisal and the employee wasn't very talkative? It can be frustrating when the other person doesn't respond to your questions. Before we place the responsibility totally on the other person we might want to consider the types of questions we generally ask. They can significantly influence the responses we get and the amount of information we obtain. There are four basic types of questions we should be familiar with when we conduct performance appraisals. They are closed, open, clarifying, and leading/loaded questions.

Closed Questions

Closed questions are essentially designed to get a specific response. The range of possible answers is quite narrow, and can be answered usually with a single word, simple phrase, or a yes/no response.

Some examples of closed questions are:

"Did you finish the report?"
"When is the deadline date?"

"Did you hear about the RIF?"
"Do you like your job here at the agency?"

Closed questions can be used to gather specific information and can move or guide a discussion in a specific direction. The respondent is usually more aware of the response you expect when closed questions are asked.

While their use has advantages, closed questions should be used with caution. Maybe it's because we've all seen too much Perry Mason, but people tend to ask closed questions more than other types of questions. That's unfortunate because closed questions can be seen as threatening by the respondent. They can arouse defensiveness in others, they may not provide much information, and, they can create misunderstanding.

Open Questions

Unlike closed questions, open questions do not require a specific, limited answer. Instead, these questions allow for a broad range of potential response. If you want information or feelings about something, you are much more likely to get what you want if you ask open questions. To exemplify this point, consider the last question asked in the preceding section. "Do you like your job here at the agency?" If you asked your subordinate that question you might get an affirmative response (particularly if he or she has upward mobility aspirations) but you don't really have any information concerning what the employee likes about the job or what feelings he or she has. If you opened the question up you might ask, "What do you like about your job here at the agency?" This question is more likely to provide you with more information, which is what you want. Some examples of open questions are:

"What do you think will happen when the new accounting
   system comes on board?"
"What's your feeling about the new budget cuts?"
"What problems do you see occurring before October 1?"

Usually open questions provide us with more information and tend to create less defensiveness. They also allow the other person to present personal views and feelings which, in turn, leave space for more dialogue. Open questions are particularly useful in performance appraisals, counseling, or career development sessions, when you need to know the employee's feelings, concerns, and aspirations. ***Rule of thumb***—if you need information and are about to ask a closed question, stop for a second and put the word *what* in front of the question. You will find that it will increase the amount of information you receive.

What versus why questions

The distinction I am about to make may appear insignificant but it's been my experience that if you need information you are better off asking *what* rather than *why* questions. A friend of mine sells real estate in the Washington, D.C., area, and he made the distinction for me. For example, when a client looks at a house he has listed, my friend might ask his client how she likes the house, with the response being, "No, I didn't like it." The next logical question might be, "Why not?" If we take a look at that *why* question, the client might feel obligated to justify her opinion rather than provide information. *Why* questions tend to have an interrogative quality about them, particularly when there is considerable voice inflection while asking them. Rather than asking why, my friend might ask, "What is it about the house you didn't like?" This question asks for information, not necessarily a justification for an opinion. This *why* versus *what* issue could help you if you need information rather than an opinion from your employee.

Clarifying questions

Open questions tend to elicit more information, but there are times when that information needs expansion or clarification. Clarifying questions serve this purpose. Some examples of clarifying questions are:

"What happened next?"

"Could you give me an example of what you mean when you say he does sloppy work?"

"You said he has a poor attitude. Could you be more specific?"

They can be used to your advantage because they help to increase the amount of information available, help prevent misunderstanding, and increase the potential for mutual understanding. They have the additional advantage of conveying a genuine interest in the other person's point of view.

Clarifying questions are very useful when you want the other person to elaborate on a topic or situation. They are especially useful when the respondent isn't very specific in describing a situation or problem.

Leading/loaded questions

Leading/loaded questions have hidden agendas and usually ask the respondent to verify or agree with a position already taken by the questioner. They are seldom effective because they tend to arouse emotional and defensive responses in others.

"Don't you agree the proposal is a good one?"
"I'm sure you won't miss another deadline, will you?"
"You don't think that ridiculous plan is going to work, do you?"
"Don't you think the new budget cuts are absolutely ludicrous?"

The questioner has already drawn a conclusion and is asking for it to be verified. People tend to become defensive when asked leading or loaded questions and agreement or understanding becomes more difficult to attain. Stay away from using leading/loaded questions. Instead, concentrate on the effective use of closed, open, and clarifying questions. Table 3.1 may help you in their use.

TABLE 3.1 Question Types

Purpose	Closed	Open	Clarifying
To gather specific information.	X		X
To help eliminate misunderstanding of what answer is required.	X		X
To guide the discussion toward a specific problem.	X		X
To give the other person a clear idea of what you want to know from him or her.	X		X
To give the other person more control of the conversation.		X	
To get information without potentially creating defensiveness.		X	
To allow the other person to express a personal point of view.		X	
To leave room for the interaction to branch out and possibly increase information gathering.		X	
To help find out what the other person sees as important in a situation.		X	X
To refrain from prematurely revealing your own beliefs about something.		X	
To promote more information.			X
To help prevent misunderstanding.			X
To clarify points which have been made.	X		X
To ensure that the meaning of the words expressed is mutually understood.	X	X	X
To show interest in the other person's comments.		X	X

In the exercise below, closed questions will be presented. In the space provided, write a corresponding open question, then the corresponding clarifying question, allowing the person who answers greater freedom to respond:

1. Do you think the new GS-9 is going to be a good worker?

Open:

Clarifying:

2. Do you dislike the new performance appraisal form?

Open:

Clarifying:

3. Do you think you qualify for that position?

Open:

Clarifying:

4. Are you going to implement plan A?

Open:

Clarifying:

5. Is it important that the budget request is finished by the scheduled deadline?

Open:

Clarifying:

6. Do you think what Senator Jones did was wrong?

Open:

Clarifying:

7. Do you think this agency will have many RIF's?

Open:

Clarifying:

In summary, remember to use open and clarifying questions when seeking information, feelings, and attitudes. They are far more effective than closed questions.

ACTIVE LISTENING SKILLS

After you have asked appropriate questions which elicit information, feelings, and attitudes, your reaction to the employee's responses is critical to developing a constructive dialogue. In particular, each participant must listen well to the other for anything productive to occur. This is more difficult than one might assume. To be effective, both participants, but particularly the supervisor, must listen actively rather than passively. Being an active listener means using the skills of paraphrasing, reflecting feelings, reflecting meaning, summarizing, and nonverbal responses.

Paraphrasing

Paraphrasing is a brief response which conveys the essence of the other's message content in the listener's own words.

When we paraphrase the content of the other person's message we are making a sincere effort to listen and understand what is being said. Actually, it is a very respectful way to respond to someone and it allows for more mutual understanding to take place. Paraphrasing is not a normal reaction. As human beings, we often react to someone's comment prematurely without fully understanding what was being said. Paraphrasing can preclude those reactions and will help keep the dialogue focused. **Rule of thumb**—When the employee makes an important statement that needs to be clearly understood by both parties, paraphrase the statement before reacting with an opinion of your own. This very important skill of paraphrasing can have significant impact on your effectiveness as a communicator—and as a manager. The following are examples of paraphrasing:

> "If I understand you correctly, you would like to have that particular sick-leave policy changed."
>
> "What I'm hearing is that you want more feedback from me concerning the project's status."

Reflecting feelings

Reflecting is a brief response which conveys the essence of the other's feelings in the listener's own words. When we reflect we are making a sincere effort to empathize with the feelings of the other person, and it is a very respectful way of responding to someone who is upset. **Rule of thumb**—When an employee expresses concern over something and is clearly upset, reflect what you think he or she is feeling before asking questions or giving an opinion. The following are examples of reflecting:

JIM: "I was so sure I'd be promoted by now. I don't know what to do."

SUPERVISOR: "It must be discouraging after you've worked this long."

MARY: "I've been working overtime for the last month, and do you think anyone even cares?"

SUPERVISOR: "Sounds like you're pretty frustrated and no one notices your effort."

It is important to remember that true reflection of feelings paraphrases what you sense others to be feeling. It is not telling the other person what he or she should feel. Some effective introductory phrases are: "Sounds like you feel————" or "Seems like you feel————."

Reflecting feelings can be very helpful, particularly when used as an immediate response to someone's expression of anger or emotional concern. It generally conveys a sincere attempt to empathize with those feelings, and will often help in their resolution or mollification. If you can't respond genuinely to the other person's feelings don't even attempt to respond that way. But, if you want to make a sincere attempt to respond, focus on the following four things:

1. Concentrate on the emotional words used.
2. Listen to the content of the message.
3. Observe the sender's nonverbal behavior.
4. Try to empathize by asking yourself, "If I were this person, what would I be feeling?"

Reflecting Meaning

When we join feelings to content in a concise paraphrase, we are reflecting meanings. Feelings are often triggered by certain events. When we reflect meanings, we are focusing both on the feelings as well as the events. The following are examples:

EMPLOYEE: "My supervisor keeps asking me if I've finished the project yet. I wish he'd quit bugging me."

Reflection of Meaning: "Sounds like you feel annoyed because your supervisor is always checking on you."

EMPLOYEE: "My boss is driving me crazy. One day he says I'm doing great and the next, he blows his top over some minor detail."

Reflection of Meaning: "Sounds like you feel confused because he seems inconsistent."

Reflecting meanings is essentially putting the skills of paraphrasing and reflecting feelings together. Respond by using, "Sounds like you feel . . . because . . . ." The expression of the feeling word followed by a *because* message will help you in developing this very important skill.

Summarizing

Summarizing is a brief summation of the main themes, points, events, feelings, expressed during the conversation. These summarizing responses will often connect a number of recent comments, or emphasize certain expressed feelings or points, by concisely paraphrasing them. While summarizing is a form of paraphrasing, it differs in that it covers *all* the key issues or points that have taken place in the conversation up to that point; it is not limited to a response to what has just been said. The following are some examples of a manager summarizing:

> "Let's go over what we have up to this point. You're saying . . . . I'm saying . . . .
> "OK Dave, let me see if I understand the steps you intend to follow on the new project. First, you are going to . . . ."
> "It's my understanding that you intend to be at work on time, from now on, but if there is a problem or emergency, you'll call me personally no later than 7:30 so we can make the necessary schedule adjustments . . . ."

During performance appraisals, when a number of issues may be covered, it is particularly necessary to summarize periodically, in order to increase the likelihood of shared expectations and understanding. If it is not done in appraisal sessions, expectations will often be violated. Summarizing can enable both the manager and subordinate to gather various comments, ideas, issues, feelings, etc., into meaningful, coherent, unified statements. Summarizing can be helpful in highlighting important areas, or can be used when a conversation is at a stalemate, and neither party can agree. It can often present a clearer perspective of each person's view. Summarizing is also useful in establishing a starting point in an appraisal or meeting, as well as a way of drawing the session to a close by tying loose ends together.

Nonverbal Responses

Nonverbal responses fall under the categories of *giving* and *receiving*. When you give nonverbal responses, you are confirming for the other person that you are listening to what he or she is saying. These confirming behaviors may take the form of head nods, smiles, raised eyebrows, leaning forward in your chair, maintaining good eye contact, etc. Generally, effective giving of nonverbal responses are those behaviors which say to the employee, "I am genuinely interested in what you are saying." Remember, if there is a disparity between what we say verbally and what we say nonverbally, the other person will, in all probability, believe the nonverbal messages over the verbal ones.

The second category of nonverbal responses, receiving, consists of our observing the nonverbal behaviors of the employee, and doing one of two things; responding to them or merely noting them silently. As managers, we can be sensitive to our impact on subordinates by observing nonverbal reactions and cues. But if you choose to respond, you need to be careful how you do it. If you sense a nonverbal reaction which needs some clarification, I suggest doing the following procedure:

1. Identify the emotion conveyed in the response and examine your own previous comments.

2. Quietly tell the employee what you observed and what your interpretation is of the observation—being sure to use a tentative statement in describing your observation; e.g., My guess is . . . ." or, "I get the feeling . . . ."

3. Ask the employee to clarify the meaning of what you've observed.

The following discussion is an example of how you might respond to a nonverbal cue:

MANAGER: "OK, we've covered the critical elements. Are you clear on them?" (Notice this is a closed question.)

EMPLOYEE: "Yes." (His/her facial gestures and hesitancy in the voice don't correspond with the verbalized response.)

MANAGER: "I know you said 'yes' but I get the feeling we're not in complete agreement. What do we need to discuss at this point?"

Responding nonverbally by being sensitive to giving and receiving can increase your communication effectiveness, particularly during performance appraisals. Look at the two examples of nonverbal responses below and write in the space provided what you think the manager should do.

Example 1
The manager has invited the employee in to discuss his/her performance. As they talk, the manager accepts a phone call, rustles through some papers on the desk, jots down a few words as if he had just thought of something, and tends to sit with legs crossed, looking at the ceiling periodically, while forming his hands in the form of a steeple.

Nonverbal Response _____

Giving _____

_____

_____

Example 2

MANAGER: "I feel pretty good about our progress here, Jim. We've identified the critical elements and developed the performance standards. If things progress as expected, you should have no problem getting the promotion soon."

EMPLOYEE: "Uh huh." (Lack of eye contact and voice tone indicate possible disbelief that anything will happen.)

Nonverbal Response _____

Receiving _____

_____

_____

Table 3.2 may help you identify times when you could use the active listening techniques.

In summary, the effective combination of appropriate questioning and active listening techniques can make your efforts considerably more productive during the performance appraisal, for both parties. Listening skills produce greater understanding and direction toward achieving mutual goals and expectations.

MANAGING DIFFERENCES

You may be saying to yourself: "All these skills are fine, but what if the employee doesn't agree with my evaluation? Then what?" Of course, there are no guarantees for success, but there are alternatives you may not have considered before. If you find that the employee disagrees with your evaluation, I would consider the following steps:

1. Treat the employee with positive regard
   a. Ask open and clarifying questions
   b. Listen actively
   c. Summarize the way you and the employee see the explicit nature of the difference

TABLE 3.2 Active Listening Skills

Purpose	Paraphrasing	Summarizing	Nonverbal responding	Responding to feeling	Responding to meaning
To help establish a starting point in a meeting where the issues have been previously discussed.		X			
To clarify a possible meaning of the reaction.	X		X	X	X
To help determine if a person's reactions and words convey the same message.	X		X	X	X
To get more information.	X		X	X	X
To help the others understand they are reacting to what is being said.	X		X	X	X
To encourage a more open level of communiction.	X		X	X	X
To uncover possible hidden problems or confusion.	X		X	X	X
To encourage a more open level of communication.	X		X	X	X
To demonstrate your understanding of how the other person feels.	X		X	X	X
To increase the probability of obtaining more information.	X		X	X	X
To help vent emotions so that they have less influence in problem-solving discussions.			X	X	X
To promote more rational discussions.	X	X	X	X	X
To check your understanding of what the other person said.	X				
To ensure that your points are being understood by the other person.	X		X		
To diminish any unintended meanings which the speaker is unaware of.	X		X	X	X
To demonstrate your interest in what the other person is saying.	X		X	X	X
To diminish the "he doesn't understand" feeling.	X		X	X	X
To help the other person think about what's been said.	X		X	X	X
To encourage the other person to explain more fully if needed.	X		X	X	X
To show that you understand what's being said.	X	X		X	X
To highlight what has already been covered and eliminate unnecessary rehashing.		X			
To keep you aware of what is important.	X	X	X	X	X
To aid in moving into new areas of discussion.		X	X	X	X

2. Differentiate your view from the employee's view
   a. Acknowledge why the employee might see the situation the way he or she does
   b. If possible, break the difference down to key issues
   c. Deal with one issue at a time
   d. Ask employee for his/her understanding of performance standards and expectations
   e. Use specific examples and data to help express your view
   f. Compare examples and data with performance standards
   g. Ask the employee to paraphrase his/her understanding of your views
   h. Be open to new information
3. Strive for agreement
   a. Try not to force your view on the employee
   b. Hold the employee responsible for his or her own performance
   c. Separate areas you agree on from those you disagree on. Emphasize areas of agreement but don't avoid dealing with the differences
   d. Reestablish performance expectations for yourself as well as the employee
   e. Develop a plan by which future perceptions can be checked and clarified

ASSERTING YOURSELF NONDEFENSIVELY

One of the most important skills you can learn from dealing with differences in the performance appraisal is asserting yourself nondefensively. Every manager must request performance changes from their employees. If an employee is not performing according to expectations, it will be necessary for you to confront the employee, discover what the problem is, resolve the problem mutually, and reassert your performance expectations—without creating a defensive climate. When you must assert yourself, therefore, there are essentially four steps to follows: (1) describe the events, (2) express the effects of the events, (3) express your feelings about the events and their consequences, and (4) reassert your expectations.

Describe the Events

Be sure that in your description of the performance deficiency you only describe the employee's behavior; don't simultaneously evaluate the employee's worth. Example: "Jim, you've been late for work six times in two weeks"; not "Jim, you're not very concerned about the job. . . ."

Express What the Effects Are

After you've described what you've been observing, describe what you see the effect to be, again without evaluating the employee's worth. Example: "When this happens, Jim, it creates problems with meeting deadlines and coordinating other activities. I also think it may be affecting the morale of the other employees"; not "Jim, you're screwing up the operation here. If it weren't for you. . ."

Express Your Feelings

This step is particularly important. The way to determine how to approach the employee is to first determine who *owns* the problem, and then decide on the message to convey.

Problem ownership   Who owns the problem concerning Jim? The supervisor? Or Jim? To get the answer, ask who is feeling the anxiety from the behavior? In this case, the supervisor owns the problem. He is the one who is being upset by Jim's tardiness. Once problem ownership is determined, the supervisor can then decide what message to use.

I and you messages   I messages tell the other person what effect his or her behavior is having on you, and they should be used by the person owning the problem. You messages should be used only if the other person owns the problem and should take the form of the reflective messages described previously. **Rule of thumb**—If I own the problem (feel anxiety from someone's behavior) use I messages. If the other person owns the problem (feels the anxiety) you messages can be used reflectively. Let's go back to the example of Jim's lateness, and see how it can be approached. If I were the supervisor and used a you message when I owned the problem, I might sound like this: "Jim, you've been late six times in two weeks. You're really screwing up, do you know that? You've been here long enough to know the rules, you should know better. Now you're going to have to shape up. You ought to be more careful . . ." You should, you better, you oughta! If you are looking for a sure way to create barriers, using you messages when you're the one who owns the problem is hard to beat. Let's try it again using I messages instead: "Jim, I'm concerned about something, and I'd like to talk about it. According to my records, you've been late six times in two weeks. I want you to know what effect that has on me and the department. I have a hard time meeting deadlines, getting the work coordinated, and I think it's having an adverse effect on the other employees. I've got a real problem with this, Jim. I'm concerned, and even a bit angry over it, but before we can deal with it, I need to know what's causing the lateness . . . ." If you had your choice, which approach would you prefer if you were in Jim's shoes? Which do you think is likely to get results?

Remember, step three is expressing your feelings. Be careful how you do it.

Reassert your expectations

After you've expressed your feelings concerning the situation, you are in a better position to reassert or modify your expectations of the employee's performance. Again, describe rather than evaluate. Example: "OK, Jim. From now on, I expect you to be on time unless an emergency occurs. If that happens, you will call before work to let me know and help me plan the day's activities"; not "OK, Jim, you're going to start being more dependable."

Being assertive, expecting high performance standards, and confronting the employee constructively by using I messages can greatly increase your effectiveness as a manager. Follow the steps. They'll pay off for you.

COACHING AND COUNSELING OTHERS

Now that we know the questioning, listening, and assertion skills, let's apply them to the coaching and counseling situations you face in your role as a manager. Coaching refers to any job-related discussion that is skill or performance related. If, during the performance-related discussion, you discover that feelings about co-workers or personal matters are an essential part of the problem to be resolved, then the discussion focuses more on counseling the employee.

A GENERIC COMMUNICATION SKILLS MODEL FOR COACHING AND COUNSELING EMPLOYEES

When you coach or counsel employees, you will find there are various generic communication skills that apply directly. Effective coaching and counseling goes through four distinct phases: contact, exploration of the problem, resolution and action planning, and finally, disengagement. Each phase has its own characteristics and skills, which, if applied, can increase your managerial effectiveness considerably. Let's take a look at the model and the associated skills for each phrase, which are described in Table 3.3.

TABLE 3.3   *Communication Skills for Coaching and Counseling*

Phase	Skills

Phase 1—Contact
Goals:
  Respect
  Rapport
  Trust
  Clear Expectations
	Nonverbal responding Using of nonverbal responses which convey to the employees that you are interested and are listening to what is being said; being aware of the nonverbal cues conveyed by the employee and responding to them if necessary
	Genuine, positive regard The use of specific non-judgmental words; conveying a genuine warmth for the employee's welfare

Phase 2—Exploration
Goals:
  Information
  Insight
  Understanding
  Empathy
	Specificity Picking out concrete elements in the employee's message and reflecting them; moving the employee away from vague generalities by requesting specific feelings, experiences, and behaviors
	Questioning Using open, clarifying, and sometimes closed questions, to allow full exploration of the problem
	Immediacy Using "here and now" reactions between you and the employee; discussing your immediate feeling or reaction to the present counseling situation
	Self-disclosure Sharing previous experiences and observations with the employee; expressing empathy because of similar shared experience
	Paraphrasing Responding by putting the content of the employees message in your own words
	Reflecting Paraphrasing your understanding of the employee's feelings and meanings
	Confronting Presenting the employee with inconsistencies in his/her behavior or thinking; to be effective, this skill must be conveyed tentatively so the employee can reevaluate and accept ownership of the problem
	Summarizing A brief summation of main themes, points, events, and feelings expressed during the conversation

Phase 3—Resolution
  and action planning
Goals:
  Problem definition
  Problem ownership
  Action plans
  Mutual expectations
	Stating the problem The precise statement of the problem as seen by the employee and manager; a mutual understanding and definition of what the problem is
	Action planning The collaborative process of developing realistic action plans; the development of mutual expectations and goals

Phase 4—Disengagement
Goals:
  Affirmation
  Respect
  Rapport
  Trust
	Focusing Commenting on the demonstrated stengths of the employee, both past and present
	Acknowledging Expressing appreciation to the employee for taking an active, collaborative part in the discussion

This generic communication skills model helps outline a process for effective interpersonal problem solving, particularly as it relates to such supervisor/employee transactions as performance appraisals, coaching/counseling sessions, and career guidance discussions.

PROVIDING CAREER GUIDANCE TO OTHERS

More and more, your job as manager requires not only technical expertise but increased expertise in managing human potential. Besides being able to create a motivating environment, appraise performance, and coach and counsel employees, you also must be able to help your employees develop their own career objectives. The major focus of performance appraisals is on past behaviors that lead to future expectations. Career guidance discussions, on the other hand, focus on future behaviors based on the analysis of the present.

The following list of questions has been distilled from interviews with over two hundred employees at all levels in the General Accounting Office (GAO). The questions cluster around three areas of concern for anyone wishing to examine his or her career development. They should also prove to be useful questions for you to ask your employees during career development discussions.

Starting where you are now

1. What do you like and dislike about your present job? (List anything that comes to mind which might be significant.)
2. What do you do well in, in your present job? What do you need to improve in, at your present job?
3. Outside of your present position, what do you enjoy, and get satisfaction from? (List things such as skills, special interest areas, hobbies, etc.) What don't you enjoy?

Exploring your ideal alternatives

1. Without leaving it, how could your present position be changed (or how could you change the way you do it) to include more that you enjoy?
2. How could it be changed to reduce or eliminate time spent on things you don't enjoy?

3. What other positions, in or out of the organization, are you qualified for, now, that might suit you better?

4. What other positions or careers should you prepare for?

Exploring ways to get there—opportunities and constraints

1. What preparation, skills, or experience do you need to pursue any of your career alternatives?

2. How can your present position be used or developed to give you needed experience and skills?

3. What other resources could you take advantage of? Educational or training programs? Coaching/counseling from supervisors or other sources? Professional counseling?

4. What personal conditions or constraints affect your ability to take advantage of the opportunities you've identified? Are you willing and able to relocate? How does your family feel about your alternatives? How much money do you need, or want, presently? In the future?

5. What career development actions can you take on your own initiative? What action can you take only with the interest and support of others in the organization?

In this chapter, the specific communication skills needed by managers were discussed. Consciously practice the skills while dealing with on-the-job situations. You'll find they'll work for you if you make a conscious effort to develop them.

REFERENCES

O'Connell, S. E. 1979. *The manager as communicator.* San Francisco, Harper & Row.

Running Effective Meetings

TO: Reader
FR: Author
RE: Chapter 4

This chapter will help you be more effective in your meetings. You'll be exploring the following topics:

1. Types of group meetings

2. Leadership functions

3. Checklists and procedures for group meetings

4. Meeting report forms

5. Procedures for the problem-solving meeting

We all participate in meetings—some of us may feel we spend too much time in them. Over the last five years, I've asked approximately fifteen hundred federal employees (first and mid-level supervisors) how much time they feel they spend in meetings while at work. The average percentage of time spent by those employees questioned, was 56 percent, more than half their time. Imagine! I also asked two follow-up questions concerning the meetings they attended. The first was, how many they considered to be beneficial in getting their jobs done. The answer was that only 20 percent of the meetings attended were considered to be beneficial! The other question was, why they felt the meetings were unproductive. The following reasons are typical:

Weak leadership.
Don't know what the goals of the meeting are.
Meetings run longer than time allotted.

Don't know why I was asked to attend.
Don't know what material I need in preparation for meeting.
People don't listen to one another.
Everyone's got a hidden agenda.
Meetings are chaotic. There's no control over procedures.
No opportunity to give my opinion. I might as well be sent a
  memo.
We have heated arguments which lead us off the topic.
Doesn't seem to be much in the meeting's objective.
The people who have the most information about the problem
  often aren't asked to attend the meeting.
We just seem to go around in circles.

To those who have spent much time in meetings, none of this is news. We have expressed or heard these sentiments before. The purpose of this chapter is to offer some insight and skills for dealing with the problems that arise when people have a meeting.

First, we'll take a brief look at the different types of meeting groups formed in organizations, and their purposes. Second, we will identify task-oriented and people-oriented leadership skills for meetings. Third, we'll apply those specific skills to familiar meeting situations. Fourth, a checklist of pre-meeting activities, conducting the meetings, and post-meeting activities will be provided for you to use on the job.

TYPES OF GROUP MEETINGS

Every government organization, regardless of its size or objective, gets work done by using group meetings. These task-oriented groups can be classified by type and function:

Executive Groups

1. Comprised of executives, directors, upper echelon personnel.
2. Has formal authority and legal liability in major policy decisions.

Representative Groups

1. Comprised of individuals who represent other groups from within or outside the organization.
2. Formed to ensure that adequate consideration is given to their constituencies.

3. Commissions, coordinating committees, labor/management committees are examples of these groups.

Standing Committees

1. Comprised of individuals who manage ongoing programs or perform standard functions.
2. Membership usually rotates periodically, but the committee exists on a permanent basis because the functions assigned to it are performed on a regular basis. EEO committees are examples of this type of formal task group.

Task Forces

1. Comprised of individuals whose task is to accomplish a single, fixed goal, or to complete a project. It's also, often called an ad hoc committee.
2. When the goal is reached, and the mission accomplished, the group dissolves.
3. A written report usually accompanies the goal achieved. Task forces are often formed to coordinate the implementation of new organizational procedures.

Investigative Groups

1. Comprised of individuals who investigate a situation, report their findings, and usually render recommendations and judgments.
2. Grievance and hearing committees are examples of these types of formal task groups.

Another way of looking at group meetings is to view them as having the following goals: (1) to provide information, (2) to provide instruction—in looking at meetings from the standpoint of their goals, it becomes clear that the role of the leader changes as a function of the meeting's goals and (3) to solve problems or make decisions.

Information-Giving Meetings　The meeting leader's role is to:

- Set clear, realistic meeting objectives
- Prepare appropriate information for the participants
- Inform participants on logistics of the meeting, its objectives, and what they need to prepare

- Present information clearly, using all available means of support, so it will be understood by all participants
- Answer questions from the participants

Instructional Meeting   The meeting leader's role with respect to the first three functions listed above remains the same. In addition, it is the instructional leader's function to:

- Present information clearly, and to demonstrate functions or skills through various audio/visual support material
- Allow participants to practice functions or skills, if possible
- Provide feedback on participant performance
- Answer questions from participants
- Provide expectations for future performance

Problem-Solving or Decision-Making Meetings   The meeting leader's role is again the same regarding the first three functions. In addition, the leader:

- Presents the problem clearly and facilitates its definition so it is mutually understood
- Facilitates group participation by asking questions, clarifying, giving information, dealing with the interpersonal dynamics of the meeting, summarizing, and listening attentively to others

It is worth noting again, that the first three steps are the same regardless of the meeting's goal. The remainder of the steps changes significantly, however, depending on the goals of the meeting. The leader's role changes from an information giver, to a teacher/trainer, to a facilitator/catalyst. The participants' roles also change from passive to active depending on the goals of the meeting.

LEADERSHIP FUNCTIONS

The difficulty in leading groups usually increases during problem-solving/decision-making meetings. The necessary skills focus on two major elements: task functions and people functions. The difficulty of implementing those functions increases because the leader, to be successful, must relinquish enough overall control and authority to get the group to participate, while maintaining enough procedural control to direct the group toward the meeting's objective.

   Let's now take a look at the specific task and people functions (Benne & Sheats 1949) necessary for effective leadership. Each function is used at different times to get the work done, and to deal with the interpersonal dynamics of the meeting. The extent to which each function may be used, varies as a function of the meeting's purpose, the characteristics of the problem, and the stage of discussion.

Task Functions

Initiating Proposing tasks or goals; defining a group problem; suggesting a procedure or ideas for solving a problem

Information or opinion seeking Requesting facts; providing relevant information about a group concern; asking for suggestions and ideas

Information or opinion giving Offering facts; providing relevant information about group concern; stating a belief; giving suggestions or ideas

Clarifying or elaborating Interpreting or reflecting ideas and suggestions; clearing up confusions; indicating alternatives and issues before the group; giving examples

Summarizing Pulling together related ideas; restating suggestions after group discussion; offering a decision or conclusion for the group to accept or reject

Consensus tester Sending up trial ballons to see if group is nearing a conclusion; checking with group to see how much agreement has been reached

People Functions

Encouraging Being friendly, warm, and responsive to others; accepting others and their contributions; regarding others by giving them an opportunity for recognition

Expressing group feelings Sensing feelings, mood, relationships within the group; sharing his or her own feeling or affect with other members

Harmonizing Attempting to reconcile disagreements; reducing tensions through "pouring oil on troubled water"; getting people to explore their differences

Compromising When ideas or status are involved in a conflict, leader offers to compromise own position; admitting error; disciplining self to maintain group cohesion

Gatekeeping Attempting to keep communication channels open; facilitating the participation of others; suggesting procedures for sharing opportunity to discuss group problems

Setting standards Expressing standards for group to achieve; applying standards in evaluating group functioning and production

Assume you are a manager of a large department and you have asked your first-line supervisors to attend a problem-solving/decision-making meeting to explore the problem of low productivity in the department. Your task is to come up with a decision which effectively resolves the problem. Below are 12 situations which could happen in any meeting. As you read through each situation, you'll have a choice of three alternative actions to resolve the situation. Circle which action you feel would be most feasible for each situation, and write in the corresponding leadership function the action represents.

Situation: You've just finished stating the purpose of the meeting—to decide on a method to increase productivity in the department. What do you do now?

1. As leader, you should recommend a solution.
2. Try to find out which supervisor is to blame.
3. Define in precise terms the nature of the problem.

   Function: _____

Situation: You've defined the problem and asked if the members agree. You now want some of their ideas, but no one wants to talk. It appears they are afraid they'll be labeled as the culprit.

1. Reflect what you consider the group members' feelings to be at that moment.
2. Call on each person for his/her ideas.
3. Wait a few moments. Someone will speak up if only to break the silence.

   Function: _____

Situation: One of the group members openly criticizes the entire group. There is obvious defensiveness to the criticism.

1. Ask the group member why she or he is being so critical.
2. Change the subject diplomatically to reduce the defensiveness.
3. Ask the other group members how they feel about the criticism they've just received.

   Function: _____

Situation: Everyone in the meeting has expressed feelings and opinions about the reasons for low productivity. One of the members complains that she's tired of hearing how everyone feels and wants to see more progress in the meeting.

1. Move the discussion away from this sensitive area in order to reduce defensiveness in the group.
2. Ask the group members how they think they should proceed at this point.
3. Ask the group members for more factual information to support their opinions concerning low productivity.

   Function: _____

Situation: The group presents more opinions and factual data. One member is adamant about the cause of low productivity—a position you silently don't agree with. Group members ask for your opinion.

1. Ask the more adamant member to explain her position more fully.
2. Give the group members your own opinion, and any additional information you feel might be helpful.
3. Summarize the situation up to this point, but be sure not to express your own opinion.

   Function: _____

Situation: One of the group members openly criticizes you for the narrow approach you have taken to identify a single cause for the problem of low productivity. He feels there may be more than one reason for the problem. The other group members are looking at you, to see how you will react to their criticism.

1. Defend your position. Remember you are the meeting leader.
2. Communicate your reasoning again, so the group understands the rationale for your approach.
3. Modify the approach you've taken with the problem.

   Function: _____

Situation: The meeting is going around in circles, and you, as well as the other group members, don't feel you're getting anywhere.

1. Use your authority to firmly tell the members they are beginning to repeat themselves.
2. Attempt to clarify the situation by using a flip chart to review all of the proposed alternatives presented thus far.

3. Try to get the group moving by expressing your opinion about the causes of the problem.

   Function: _____

Situation: After listing all the alternatives on a flip chart, the majority of the group agrees on the essential cause of the problem. You get a strong indication that they want to adjourn the meeting at this point.

1. Devote a few minutes to smoothing out some of the interpersonal conflicts which have occurred in the meeting.
2. Remind the group that the original purpose of the meeting was to develop a solution to the problem, and decide on a course of action.
3. Summarize the group's accomplishments thus far, and ask for proposals to solve the problem to be submitted before the next morning.

   Function: _____

Situation: One of the members of the group has considerable experience and expertise, and could make a valuable contribution to this meeting. However, she has not participated much in the meeting, because of some earlier criticism she received from another group member.

1. Ask her what's bothering her.
2. Apologize to her concerning the earlier, unwarranted criticism.
3. Give her some special recognition.

   Function: _____

Situation: Two people have gotten into a personal argument. It's become pretty heated, and the other members sitting around the table are observing, and probably wondering what you intend to do about it.

1. You decide who is right after you've asked each person to restate his or her position.
2. Ask the two people to settle their argument later—after the meeting.
3. Ask the question of the entire group, requesting them to give their opinions.

   Function: _____

Situation: The meeting has come to a standstill. The members are sharply divided over the best solution, and it appears you've reached a stalemate.

1. You should now make the decision for the group.
2. Ask the members to choose a representative from each point of view to study the proposed solution.
3. Summarize the progress made thus far, to stimulate thinking.

   Function: _____

Situation: You feel the group has come to some agreement concerning a specific course of action. You'd like the proposal to be acceptable to everyone, and also get their commitment.

1. Check with each member to see if there is a consensus.
2. Assume the group members will accept the solution, and ask for someone to volunteer.
3. Thank the group for their time and effort, and assign responsibilities and deadlines for the solution's implementation.

   Function: _____

Recommended answers

Situation	Behavior	Function
1	3	Initiating
2	1	Expressing group feelings
3	3	Gatekeeping
4	3	Information and opinion seeking
5	2	Information and opinion giving
6	3	Compromising
7	2	Clarifying
8	2	Setting standards
9	3	Encouraging
10	3	Harmonizing
11	3	Summarizing
12	1	Consensus testing

CHECKLISTS AND PROCEDURES FOR GROUP MEETINGS

Following are several checklists you can use to help you prepare for, conduct, follow up, and evaluate meetings in your organization.

Pre-meeting activities

- What is the purpose of the meeting?
- What are the things to be achieved from the meeting?
- What procedure should I use as the meeting leader?
- Who should be there? How do I view their involvement and their impact on the outcome?
- Where should the meeting be held? How long should it last? When should it be held?
- What should the participants be told before the meeting? Should they prepare anything? Should they be sent any material in advance?
- What physical details need to be attended to; room, audio-visual equipment, refreshments?
- What action should be taken after the meeting is over? Will proceedings and results be recorded and disseminated?

Conducting the meeting

Did you make an opening statement which included the purpose, procedures, and ground rules for the meeting?

Check the task and people functions you performed:

Task	Often	Seldom	Never
Initiating	_____	_____	_____
Information and opinion seeking	_____	_____	_____
Information/opinion giving	_____	_____	_____
Clarifying	_____	_____	_____
Summarizing	_____	_____	_____
Consensus testing	_____	_____	_____
People			
Encouraging	_____	_____	_____
Expressing group feelings	_____	_____	_____
Harmonizing	_____	_____	_____
Compromising	_____	_____	_____
Gatekeeping	_____	_____	_____
Evaluating	_____	_____	_____

Were you patient with differences of opinion?
Did you actively listen, by paraphrasing, and by reflecting feelings and meaning?

Were you aware of your own nonverbal behavior, as well as that
 of other members?
Did you keep the meeting on track, by maintaining appropriate
 control?
When you sought information, did you ask mostly open and
 clarifying questions?

Post-meeting activities

Was the meeting objective achieved?
What things are to be done now?

Actions _____   **Who** _____   **Target Date** _____
      _____   _____   _____
      _____   _____   _____
      _____   _____   _____

What is to be included in the memo to be disseminated to the
 meeting members? Who else should receive memo?
Is there a need for a follow-up meeting?
Should different meeting procedures be considered for future
 meetings? How effective was the procedure you chose?
Were the appropriate people there? Should there be others
 present if a follow-up meeting is necessary?
Were the physical facilities sufficient?
What three things can be done to improve the next meeting?

MEETING REPORT FORMS

Every meeting you lead should be important, otherwise it probably wasn't
necessary to hold it in the first place. To maximize your communication
effectiveness regarding meetings, I recomend you send all participants, and
other pertinent nonparticipants, a meeting report covering the following
areas:

- Organization or unit
- Date and place
- Called by
- Attendees
- Purpose of meeting
- Topics to be discussed (agenda should be attached to form)
- Actions, recommendations, responsibilities, deadlines
- General comment

PROCEDURES FOR THE PROBLEM-SOLVING MEETING

The procedure used to attack problems is, in my opinion, always the leader's. It is up to him or her to decide on the procedural format or process by which the problem is to be solved, and then to be a catalyst that helps others provide the content or information within those procedures. The following procedural formats might prove helpful to you for your next problem-solving meeting:

1. Standard procedure
   a. What are the limits and nature of the problem?
   b. What are the causes and consequences of the problem?
   c. What characteristics must an acceptable solution have?
   d. What are our alternatives?
   e. Which alternative is the best?
   f. How do we evaluate our solution?

2. Ideal solution form
   a. Are we all agreed on the nature of the problem?
   b. What would be the ideal solution from the point of view of all parties involved in the problem?
   c. What conditions within the problem can be changed, so that ideal solutions might be achieved?
   d. Of the solutions available to us, which one approximates the ideal solution?

3. PERT (Programmed Evaluation Review Techniques)
   a. What is the final event?
   b. When must it happen?
   c. What must be accomplished in order to get that final event?
   d. Diagram a sequential critical path of steps and activities to be done, with time estimates.
   e. Develop alternatives and contingency routes along the critical path.

4. Nominal group technique (Delbecq, Van de Ven, & Gustafson, 1975). The meeting leader explains the purpose of the meeting, and its procedures, defines the problem, and asks the participants to complete the following steps:
   Step 1: Each person writes down ideas, options, alternatives, and solutions privately without discussion.
   Step 2: The results of Step 1 are presented to the group by each person. These results are recorded on a flip chart. There is no discussion or evaluation of ideas during Step 2.
   Step 3: Anyone may ask for clarification of an idea or

proposed solution. There is to be no evaluation of the ideas or proposals during Step 3.

Step 4: Each person ranks the various proposed solutions privately. The results are tallied to determine the relative support for each solution.

Step 5: Discussion of the preliminary vote is conducted.

Step 6 A final vote is taken.

5. Brainstorming

The meeting leader explains the purpose of the meeting and its procedures, defines the problem, assigns a recorder, and asks the participants to adhere to the following rules:

  a. Criticism is ruled out. Evaluation of ideas must be withheld until later.

  b. The wilder the ideas, the better. Even offbeat, impractical ideas may trigger ideas in others.

  c. Quantity is wanted. The greater the number of ideas, the more likelihood of good ones.

  d. Combination and improvement are wanted. If a participant sees a way to improve on a previous idea, he or she should tell the group, so it can be recorded at once.

Brainstorming can be an extremely effective way of generating a large number of ideas in a very short period of time. After all ideas have been recorded, the group can begin prioritizing the ideas, and do further analysis.

If the communication skills and techniques covered in this chapter are used while conducting meetings, you will become a more effective manager.

REFERENCES

Benne, K. & P. Sheats. 1949. Functional roles of group members. *Journal of Social Issues* 4:41-49, in *Small group communication: A reader*, edited by Cathcart, R. S. and Samavar, L. A., Duburque, Iowa: William C. Brown, Pub., 1974.

Delbecq, A. L., A. H. Van de Ven, & D. H. Gustafson. 1975. Group techniques for program planning: A guide to nominal group and delphi processes. Glenview, Ill.: Scott Foresman.

CHAPTER 5

Public and Interagency Communication in the Government

MEMO

TO: Reader
FR: Author
RE: Chapter 5

This chapter examines the concerns and techniques for communicating with the public. In particular, you'll be exploring the following topics:

1. The perception of the government bureaucrat
2. Communication with the public
3. Conducting effective briefings
4. Teleconferencing

THE PERCEPTION OF THE GOVERNMENT BUREAUCRAT

Good communication should begin with some sensitivity to the audience's attitude toward the communicator's credibility. Perception is an important term here, because the real character of the communicator is secondary; it's the perception that matters. Credibility filters the communication experience and works to predetermine the acceptability of the message. In the case of the federal employee's communication with the general public, a punchy little term has gained popularity in defining the credibility of the communicator: *Bureaucrat!* The usual pronunciation has a distinctly negative ring to it.

The evidence supporting this ranges from that well-worn little joke—the one where the prime example of a lie is said to be, "I'm from the federal government and I'm here to help"—to the substance of recent presidential elections. The winner of the 1976 election, the *outsider*, promised to subdue the federal bureaucracy by reorganizing it. By 1980, the issue was hotter than ever with the voters, and the new axiomatic solution to bureaucracy was fewer bureaucrats. In the words of Herbert Kaufman (1981), "antibureaucratic sentiment has taken hold like an epidemic."

So what's the federal manager to do about it? In the private sector when your image is bad, you launch a major PR campaign to improve it, as in the case of the oil companies who shifted their entire advertising effort from selling gas to selling themselves. But public law prohibits agencies from conducting any public relations.

Further, the opportunities that are available to communicate with the public are highly structured, and subject to many rules inhibiting the action of federal agencies.

This chapter will look at three areas of public communication with the administrative branch of the government. The first section will look at some of the interpersonal dynamics that underlie the basic process. The next section will focus on communication skills which apply to government briefings, and outlines some rules and observations that should help the federal manager in presenting informative and persuasive briefings. The final section will focus on the effective use of teleconferencing and its implications.

COMMUNICATION WITH THE PUBLIC

Anyone who works for the government probably feels a need for help in clarifying the public perception of the bureaucrat. Several observations offer a new angle that gives some insight to how that image can be improved.

Herbert Kaufman's study on the "fear of bureaucracy" argued that the public is afraid that the activities of the executive branch agencies are too pervasive, beyond democratic controls, and that the work force is largely unproductive. He then analyzed these assertions, and found them to be loaded with bias and contradiction. For example, when critics explain that government is too pervasive in the daily life of citizens, they illustrate this with programs that benefit someone else. Programs that benefit the critics are, of course, energetically defended. Every program has its public, and Kaufman interprets this to mean that government is too responsive to its citizenry, not necessarily too pervasive.

"Beyond democratic control," is the illusion of someone who has never felt the heat of Congressional oversight, or the will of a strong president. One senator, whose appropriations committee disagreed with the activities of an agency it usually financed with lump-sum appropriations said, "We proceeded to earmark (their) budget from one end to the other. We just tied it up in knots to show that it was the Congress, after all, that dictated policy" (Kaufman 1981).

The unproductive claim is an even tougher one to make stand up. The productivity of the federal work force has grown at about the same rate as nonfarm private-sector productivity—1.2 percent versus 1.3 percent as measured in the 1966 to 1976 period. It is clear that the perception of the federal employee's power, freedom, and pace is not at all in sync with the reality.

Kaufman does not conclude that the system is without faults, or that the frustrations stimulating the criticisms are without merit. It is clear, however, that the scope of the problem exceeds the parameters of the federal agencies. He concludes that bureaucracy is a good target for social frustrations, and that the bureaucrat is the most available scapegoat. It's a simple transfer of hostility.

The bearing this has on communication goes back to the definition of credibility. It's the perception that matters, not the reality. So one might logically conclude from this, that, guilty or not, the federal employee must bear the burden of the system's problems, and that communication must always be initiated across this perceptual deficit of credibility.

But this conclusion is not the only one we can draw. There is an interesting paradox here that lightens the load. A past director of OPM, Alan Campbell, has cited two rather significant pieces of research that show that the public is of two different minds in its attitude toward federal employees. There's a discrepancy between their opinions of public servants in the aggregate, and of the individual public employees they encounter. Campbell (1978) cites studies which show, that when queried about public employees, the responses were generally, "irrational, violently assertive, and antipublic employees." But when asked about specific encounters with specific employees, it turned out that two thirds responded with favorable reactions. Another study reported by Campbell showed that the public speaks very favorably on their dealings with individual government employees. Seventy percent reported complete satisfaction with their encounter. Nevertheless, their prejudice was so firm that they concluded their experiences were the exception to the rule.

The conclusion here, is that although it is probably safe to assume that every government employee's personal communication experience is preceeded by a negative bias, it is up to each individual to reverse that image, a proposition that can be successfully carried out with a basic appreciation of interpersonal communication skills. The proper use of interpersonal communication skills can improve your image. For example, calling the government and getting the runaround, or several uninterested parties, is a common complaint. I was recently doing some work for a private firm on a task that had me calling several agencies for reports and other data. I called one agency and was impressed by polite, energetically helpful assistance from a number of people there. I commented on this to the people I was working with, all of whom were more familiar with the task of extracting information from the government.

Their response intrigued me. They said it didn't used to be that way. That agency was one of the worst you could call. Then, all of a sudden, things seemed to change. People became more friendly over the phone. Helpfulness seemed the rule, rather than the exception.

I tucked that experience away in the back of my mind, and made a point of following up on it later. As I continued my research, it became increasingly clear, that from a phone caller's point of view, this one agency definitely stood out for its courtesy. Curiosity got the best of me, so I investigated.

A coincidence of events seems to have sparked the change. One relatively small office, within the agency, had asked the training branch to develop a brief course on proper telephone management, which included the cooperation, of not only the support people, who handled most routine calls, but also that of professionals, who set the mood and follow up in the more demanding cases.

The telephone training course was developed as requested. Coincidently, the Office of the President responded to newspaper criticisms of the bureaucracy's inability to deal with simple public inquiries. The typical horror story involved rude service and endless referrals, frequently winding up with the original person, who was unable to answer the question. The president sent a memo throughout the agencies, demanding improved communication. With this stimulant, the course took on greater appeal, and was offered to many offices within this particular agency. Although there are no scientific data to establish cause and effect here, it is my strong suspicion that one manager's decision to request telephone training, coupled with the catalytic support of a presidential memo, helped transform the public presentation of one agency.

Public perception of government can be improved with some attention to basic communication skills. In addition to the suggestions and techniques of preceding chapters, you have a number of additional resources available. First, check with your organization's training branch for courses in telephone communication skills. Also, check with the phone company. The Bell Systems in many cities offer short courses on how to improve telephone use in business communication. Telephone communication skills are only part of the picture. How well you present yourself face-to-face in a public context, has significant impact on your agency's image.

CONDUCTING EFFECTIVE BRIEFINGS

Public briefings are another way that you represent your agency. As a practicing supervisor, or manager, I'm sure you've been asked to attend and give briefings. When you attend them, do you often find them to be too technical or too elementary; rambling, unclear, or unstructured; are they hampered by ineffective visual aids? When you are requested to give a briefing, do you find it difficult to plan and organize? Are you unsure of techniques to make the briefing clear to everyone? Are you aware of the appropriate visual aids to use? If you have these concerns, this section may help you deal with them. The following simple steps will help put you on the right track toward an effective briefing:

Step 1   Develop realistic objectives   One of the first questions to ask yourself is: "Why am I giving this briefing? Is it to inform, instruct, or persuade?"

Step 2   Determine the results wanted from this briefing   Once you determine your objectives, you need to look at the short-term result you want from the briefing. For example, the Environmental Protection Agency might have a program which is to reduce the amount of hazardous pollutants in coal producing areas. The result of your briefing might be to get funding for the program's research and development phase.

Step 3   Identify the audience   This is a critical step in any briefing. It is extremely important if you can, to determine your audience's knowledge level, their opinion toward you or your agency, their reasons for attending the briefing, and whether they are in a position to make or significantly influence a decision.

Step 4   Develop the briefing plan   This step can be developed more easily by answering the following 10 questions:

1. What is the title of your briefing? (By forcing yourself to develop a title, you can focus more directly on your objective.)
2. Where/when is the briefing to be held?
3. What support facilities do you need? (Room requirements, coffee, seating, lighting, etc.)
4. Who asked for the briefing?
5. What political/practical issues are there for this briefing? (What effect might this briefing have on the audience, and more particularly, on you and your influence or stature in the organization?)

6. What are your objectives for this briefing? (What results do you want to have if the briefing is successful?)

7. Who is your audience? (What is their knowledge of the subject; their position toward the subject; their organizational position?)

8. What are your main points? (These consist of the major ideas you want your audience to retain if the briefing is successful.)

9. What verbal supporting material is needed for each main point?

10. What visual aids would be most effective?

Step 5 *Develop the verbal supporting materials* The verbal supporting materials can take numerous forms. The following list of options may be helpful:

Examples
Illustrations (Detailed example)
Specific instances (Undeveloped examples)
Statistics
Expert testimony
Personal experience
Analogy (Comparing two different things and pointing out their similarities)

Step 6 *Organize the material* There are a number of ways to logically organize the material for the briefing. The following are a few which may be helfpul:

Chronological order—Particularly useful when reviewing historical information or when describing sequential steps in a process. For example, a briefing might develop the chronology of the Trident Submarine program, or describe the steps necessary to get a piece of legislation passed in the Congress.
Spatial order—Useful when describing spatial differences, similarities, characteristics of things. For example, a briefing at the National Oceanic and Atmospheric Administration (NOAA) might describe the spatial order of the different atmospheric levels.
System/subsystem order—Very useful when describing the structural characteristics of things. For example, a briefing might refer to the United States government as consisting of three major parts: the executive branch, legislative branch, and judical branch.

Problem-solving advantages—This order presents a problem, suggests a solution, and shows how significant advantages will acrue from the solution. For example, a briefing at the Environmental Protection Agency (EPA) might show how certain gases are affecting the ozone layer, and recommend a ban on the gases with obvious advantages occurring from their elimination.

Step 7   Organize the briefing   Now that you've gone through the first six steps, you need to put it all together. I'm going to suggest a straightforward structure that will help in putting your ideas together in a logical manner. Very simply, the briefing can be organized under the standard introduction, body, and conclusion format. Let's look at each section and make specific suggestions for each:

> **Introduction**   Here are some ways to introduce your briefing:
> Reference to the occasion
> Introduce self and/or agency
> State purpose and give an overview of your main points (This is critical. I recommend this be done within the first minute of your briefing.)
> Show why the topic is relevant for the audience
> Cite an example, illustration, specific instance, quote, or statisics to get the audience's attention.
> **Body**   Once you've stated the purpose and given an overview of your main points, the body of the briefing should be constructed by (1) stating each main point, (2) supporting each main point with evidence and/or visual aids, (3) internally summarizing each main point, and (4) making a smooth transition to the next main point.
> **Conclusion**   The conclusion should always contain at least two elements: (1) a summary, and (2) a final appeal to the audience. Many of the same techniques used in the introduction can also be used in the conclusion of your briefing.

The completed briefing might take the following form:

Introduction

Purpose: "The purpose of this briefing is to . . ."
Relate topic to the audience: "This information is particularly important because . . ."
Overview: "I'm going to cover the following . . ."
Transition: "Let's consider the first point . . ."

Body
First Main Point

Support material:
Internal summary: "So we can see that a serious problem exists . . ."
Transition: "Let's see what can be done about it . . ."

Second Main Point

Support material:
Internal summary: "So we can see that the proposal is both workable and practical. . ."
Transition: "Let's consider the specific advantages developing from this proposal . . ."

Third Main Point

Support Material:
Internal summary: "These advantages will have a far-reaching effect . . ."
Transition: "Let's review what's been covered . . ."

Conclusion

Brief summary of each main point:
Final appeal to the audience and concluding remarks.

Step 8 *Develop your visual aids* There are a number of useful visual aids available to you. I've chosen the ones most commonly used in government briefings:

1. Charts (e.g., organizational charts, flow charts, bar graphs, pie graphs, etc.)

Advantages	*Disadvantages*
Inexpensive	Can be easily displaced
Can be done quite pro-fessionally and easily	Inconvenient to store
Easy to use	Can be difficult to handle
	Can be too small for large audiences

2. Overhead Projector
(Projects onto a screen for a transparency)

Advantages	*Disadvantages*
Inexpensive	Requires a special process
Can face the audience while using them	for making transparencies
Can look very professional	
Allows for flexibility	
Room can remain lit	

3. Slide Projector

Advantages	*Disadvantages*
Very useful for brief-	Slide preparation can be
ings which require many	expensive
visual aids	
Easily operated	
Speaker is in total	
control, and can flexibly	
move forward or backward	
while maintaining contact	
with audience	

4. Video Tape

Advantages	*Disadvantages*
Very flexible	Very expensive
Speaker is in complete	Good deal of preparation
control by using fast	Bulk/heavy
forward, rewind, and	Difficult to use with
pause buttons	large audiences, unless
Useful when motion is	multiple monitors are
required to make your	available
points more vivid	

This short section on briefing techniques should provide you with the essentials to make a successful briefing. I'd like to end with some **Rules of thumb:** (1) keep your briefings simple and to the point; (2) limit your briefing to a few essential main points; (3) always state your purpose, the relevance of the topic to the audience, and overview in your introduction; (4) always use internal summaries and transitions between your main points; and (5) always include a summary and a final appeal in your conclusion. Good luck with your next briefing!

TELECONFERENCING

Teleconferencing can be defined as three or more people, in two or more locations, communicating electronically by (1) audio-voice only, (2) audio graphics—audio plus visual support material, and (3) video. Let's take a look at some questions about teleconferencing.

Can it cut cost?   Definitely! An analysis conducted by the General Services Administration (*Performance* 1981) concluded that a one day conference in Washington, D.C., involving one participant from each of ten regions could be itemized thus:

```
Average cost of
air travel.................................................................................. $200
Per diem................................................................................... $ 75
                                                                                        ------
                                                                                        $275
Persons attending....................................................................  × 10
Minimum cost of meeting....................................................  $2,750
```

A teleconference (audio) for one hour with the same participants in ten different areas would cost approximately $150.

When is it appropriate to use teleconferencing? In a survey conducted under the auspices of the International Association of Business Communicators (O'Connell and Falcione 1982) it was found that different types of meetings are more or less appropriate for teleconferencing.

Eight hundred professional communicators from the International Association of Business Communicators (IABC) were asked what types of meetings were most appropriate for teleconferencing (video). The following shows the results of the survey.

Teleconferencing is appropriate for:

• Training and professional development
• Information sharing
• Status reporting

Teleconferencing is inappropriate for:

• Problem solving
• Decision making
• Conflict resolution

The key variable is whether two-way, fact-to-face communication is a necessary ingredient in the meeting's success. As the necessity for that ingredient increases, the utility of teleconferencing decreases.

What are some guidelines for the use of teleconferencing? Based on our data, our survey identified the following guidelines:

• Determine whether one-way or two-way transmission is best by knowing the quality and degree of interaction required.
• Keep transmission time under two hours.
• Punctuate the presentation with on-site discussion and questions.
• Choose speakers who are comfortable with, and skilled at TV or audio presentations.
• Focus speaker time on a few topics; favor intensity over diversity.

- Provide supporting visual materials.
- Design a format that encourages interaction by:
  - Limiting the number of sites to increase interaction
  - Providing a local resource/discussion leader
  - Encouraging discussion among presenters

Is there a central location for teleconferenceing available to various government agencies?   Yes! The General Services Administration (GSA) has a teleconference room (audio) at the GSA Buildng in Washington, D.C. It's a soundproofed conference center with the following features:

- High quality audio system
- Sensitivity microphones
- 25 person conference table (total room capacity 50 people)
- Podium with microphone
- Overhead projector
- Blackboards
- Conference operator present at all conferences
- Up to 28 telephones which can be connected simultaneously

The facility is available to all federal agencies who wish to take advantage of its service. Teleconferencing is definitely a communication tool worth using, if you haven't already. It can save in travel costs, reduce operating expenses, and increase productivity for your agency.

In summary, your image and the image of your agency can be significantly enhanced if you consider improving telephone and briefing skills. As you and your employees interface with the public and with other agencies, these two communication skills represent the agency, and in a sense, these skills represent to the listener, your agency's expertise and credibility.

Also, the impact of telecommunications will be great on organization functioning. Its effective use can increase your agency's efficiency, and improve its image if used properly.

REFERENCES

Campbell, A. K. 1978. Running out of esteem? *Civil Service Journal.* (January-March): 4–10.

Kaufman, H. 1981. Fear of bureaucracy: A raging pandemic. *Public Administration Review.* (Jan./Feb.): 1–9.

O'Connell, S. E. & R. L. Falcione. 1982. IABC teleconference: The results of a survey. (Research sponsored by the International Association of Business Communications).

"Travel by telephone," *Performance,* August 1981, 8.

CHAPTER 6

Communication, Productivity, and the Future of Government Service

<u>MEMO</u>

TO: Reader
FR: Author
RE: Chapter 6

Productivity is a significant issue in government organizations. This chapter examines several productivity programs in the public sector, which have been successful, mainly because of their emphasis on effective communication practices. You'll be exploring the following topics in this chapter:

1. Productivity in the private and public sectors
2. HUD's B.E.S.T. Program
3. The Quality Circle Program of the Norfolk Navy Shipyard
4. Quality circles in government
5. What makes a successful government organization?
6. Rating your own organization.

During the 1980 presidential campaign, we heard critiques of public sector productivity, and how it should be improved at all levels of government. The Reagan administration made the deepest budget cuts in this nation's history. The effects of those cuts were profoundly felt at every level of government. Agencies and programs were trying to find ways to increase productivity in a much more austere environment. Given this background, the purpose of this chapter is to examine the difference between private-and public-sector ideas of productivity; what has been done to increase productivity through effective communication systems; and what you as managers can do to improve productivity and communication in your own agencies, while dealing with decreased budgets.

PRODUCTIVITY IN THE PRIVATE AND PUBLIC SECTORS

The term *productivity* should not be defined in the same way for both private and public sectors. Blair Ewing (1980) defines private-sector productivity as the ratio of output (expressed as quantity or volume of products and services), to labor input (expressed as labor costs). He points out that productivity is traditionally viewed as a measure of efficiency. Ewing suggests that productivity for the public sector includes more than efficiency. It includes improvements in effectiveness, responsiveness, and the quality and timeliness of services and products.

Ewing further suggests that for government agencies to increase their productivity, the following procedural and substantive elements should be considered:

1. Top management needs to be committed to productivity improvement. A good approach is to issue a policy statement which sets forth what is to be done to achieve productivity improvement. Top management may decide to be more or less actively and personally involved, but its commitment must, at least, be communicated through a forceful policy statement.

2. Responsibility for overall productivity improvement should be assigned to a specific unit within the agency. That unit must be held accountable for ensuring action, collecting and organizing data, conducting analyses, developing recommendations agencywide, and disseminating information about the productivity improvement efforts. The unit need not be a new one; most agencies already have components with appropriate technical skills and perspectives.

3. The unit must be linked to related sources in and outside the agency. Units planning productivity programs need to learn about other agency efforts, about overall government productivity initiatives, and about research findings. They should inform themselves about programs such as merit pay, incen-

tive awards, employee discipline, labor relations, and other improvement programs of the budget and personnel offices.

4. Employees at every level must take part in developing ideas about how to improve work and productivity. Seek union involvement, or where there is not a union, seek employee involvement, by asking for suggestions and ideas about how to make the organization work better. Employees know a great deal about their work, and often have not been asked for their ideas.

5. Productivity improvements must be publicized. Efforts that have paid off in lower costs, higher quality, greater timeliness, and more effectiveness can inspire others. Many in the government still must be persuaded that improvements can be made, and the most convincing evidence is the actual performance of others engaged in similar functions. Once the procedural elements are established, turn your attention to the equally important substantive elements in your productivity improvement programs.

6. Define the mission of the agency. The mission should be defined in terms of services to be provided—to whom, toward what end, at what cost, in what time frame, and with what long and short-range goals and objectives in mind.

7. Establish indicators, measures, and a measurement system. Integrate it with management information systems already used in decision making. The measurement system must be tied to the mission and objectives, and must give managers information on the performance of the organization compared with its objectives. It must measure work activity as well as productivity, and it must be designed to use in making decisions about staffing levels, budget justification, and performance appraisal.

8. Analyze the measurement data and transmit the data and the analysis to managers. Using both the data and other techniques of organization assessment, the analysis must explain what has occurred over time within the agency and its subordinate units.

9. Develop recommendations to improve productivity. The recommendations should be actions to improve the substantive work processes and results within the agency, but they should also include actions to improve the use of technology, capital investment, and individual performance.

These nine elements constitute a framework for a productivity program; others may be added. Some may warrant less attention than others in your particular organization. All of them deserve consideration.

Mr. Ewing's procedural and substantive elements for a successful productivity program are extremely useful for the practicing managers at local, state, and federal agencies. Now let's take a look at some of the productivity programs which have been implemented in government agencies. I've chosen the ones which I feel have particular implications concerning more effective communication systems.

DEPARTMENT OF HOUSING AND URBAN DEVELOPMENT (HUD) BEHAVIORAL ENGINEERING SYSTEMS TRAINING (B.E.S.T.) PROGRAM

HUD's B.E.S.T. program is an excellent example of how many of these concepts we have been discussing can be implemented. The program combines performance measurement, a strong emphasis on supervisory feedback, and performance recognition. Operating with rewards other than cash, the program has resulted in significant productivity improvements in HUD's Office of Finance and Accounting.

The major impetus for doing something about productivity came from findings revealed on OPM's Federal Employee Attitude Survey. It was found that:

- Employees did not have specific, quantitative, individual goals to let them know exactly what their supervisors expected of them.
- Employees did not have an immediate feedback system to let them know how they were performing in comparison to a standard. They received annual reviews but had little immediate feedback information indicating acceptable or unacceptable performance.
- There was no dependable mechanism to evaluate and reinforce good performance. Consequently, employees didn't receive recognition for good work. They felt they were noticed only when they made mistakes.
- Employees were judged on their good attitudes, cooperation, and initiative, qualities which were inferential, subjective, and difficult to measure.

In reaction to the above employee perception, the B.E.S.T. program was started in 1979. It can be broken down into four phases: training, analysis, feedback, and consequence management (which ensures that good performance is recognized and poor performance is assisted and rectified). Table 6.1 on the following pages shows the four steps followed in the program.

The HUD program is a major success. For example, the assigned Home Mortgage Section's accuracy rate rose from 82 percent to 92 percent in four weeks, and reached 99 percent in two months. Over a ten-week period, the unit's workload rose from seventy-eight items reviewed per week, to a peak load of twelve hundred, and still maintained an increase in accuracy.

The interesting thing about the HUD program is that the fundamental concerns centered around the communication principles emphasized in this book: (1) mutual expectations, (2) immediate and positive feedback, and (3) the use of descriptive rather than inferential language when evaluating performance.

Now let's look at another program, which in order to be effective, the supervisor and program participants must have appropriate meeting communication skills.

THE QUALITY CIRCLE PROGRAM OF THE NORFOLK NAVY SHIPYARD

Quality circles (QC's), which originated in Japan after World War II, are small groups of workers who meet voluntarily on a regular basis to identify, analyze, and solve problems experienced on the job. The size of a QC varies from three to fifteen employees from the same work area, all of whom are familiar with the problems encountered. Membership is voluntary, but once an employee joins, he or she has the responsibility to participate actively. The major objectives of QC's are to increase the quality and quantity of the goods and services provided by its members, to improve communication, and to better identify goals among the members, and within the organization.

The Norfolk Naval Shipyard, which employs approximately eleven thousand workers, started a quality circle program in 1979. The original pilot program was a major success. It contributed to $7 million in avoided costs and was directly responsible for saving over $200,000 in actual costs in its first year of operation. As of 1981, the shipyard had expanded their effort to forty-four circles. Over the next three years, they anticipate having five hundred QC's throughout the facility.

The QC program's basic structure is as follows:
A steering committee which sets the policy and goals for the program, and selects facilitators
A coordinator who oversees the daily QC operations, as well as carrying out other duties in training

TABLE 6.1   The Four Steps Followed in the B.E.S.T. Program

Training	*Analysis*
Offer instruction for supervisors and managers, in theory and practical application of a performance management system	Supervisors and managers identify outputs of work unit
Develop a list of positive reinforcers	Identify and select elements of general performance standard for improvement:
	Rate of production Accuracy Timeliness Cost Quality Completeness
	Gather baseline data on present level of performance
	Calculate costs and benefits of improving each output
	Analyze factors blocking performance

Feedback	Positive Reinforcement
Each worker records performance on simple forms	Workers receive daily reinforcement, using forms that record performance and graph trends in goal attainment
Supervisors review forms with employees, noting performance of workers	Supervisors reinforce workers for improvement in performance, and use feedback data to correct deficient performance
	Examples of some employee rewards for good performance, excluding money:
	<ul><li>Personal visit from top management</li><li>Commendations, awards, or letters from top management</li><li>Certificates</li><li>Employee mention in agency newsletter</li><li>Chance to attend higher level meetings</li><li>Desirable or more challenging assignments</li><li>Job rotation</li><li>Training/career development</li><li>Meetings or lunches with supervisor</li><li>Opportunity to advise supervisor</li><li>Mention in a memo or letter</li><li>Assignment to train others</li></ul>
	Supervisors chart progress of work unit performance
	Managers reinforce supervisors for:
	<ul><li>Monitoring and reinforcing performance of workers</li><li>Reporting performance data</li><li>Identifying and solving performance problems</li></ul>

Facilitators drawn from the ranks on one year assignments; they
present the quality circle program to new participants as well
as monitor the progress of existing circles

The quality circles themselves are composed of volunteer workers who are willing to serve on a circle for an hour each
week. Each circle has a leader who may be the supervisor for
that work unit, or someone else who provides leadership for
the group

As indicated, the Norfolk Naval Shipyard QC program has been a
major success story in public-sector production. The following factors have
played a key role in its success, and they are recommended to any QC
program.

A well-organized steering committee is helpful.

Selection of the facilitator is the most important decision in
establishing a QC program. This person must be able to work
at all levels, be creative, and above all, able to work well with
people, and be aware of the political atmosphere of the
organization.

Management support is required. Union support is desirable and
should be solicited.

The program must be voluntary, but management should provide
encouragement in establishing circles.

Circle members must feel free to work on problems they choose
to work on (within established limits).

The facilitators must keep management informed of problems
circles have selected to solve, and on the progress circles are
making in reaching solutions.

Quality, not quantity, should be the first consideration. Expansion will come of its own accord as word of mouth spreads
success stories.

Adherence to the quality concept and procedures, is mandatory
for a successful program. A major function of the facilitator is
to ensure that procedures are followed. Relaxing procedures
will cause circles to be non-productive, and eventually to
disband.

The quality circle concept has high potential for improving
quality and productivity. If not managed carefully, however,
the concept could be harmful to an organization.

Once a solution to a problem has been approved by management,
the facilitator and/or the circle leader must follow up to ensure
that it is carried out. Solutions which have been approved and
are not implemented, or are not implemented as proposed, will
destroy all gains from the program.

QUALITY CIRCLES IN GOVERNMENT

The success of QC programs in the private sector has prompted government agencies to consider using them. As of 1981, the General Accounting Office reported that 13 federal agencies—ten defense and three civil—have QC programs. The programs cover administration, maintenance, and supply and distribution; they also include employees in both general schedule and wage grade categories. It appears that quality circles are well on their way to finding their place in the public sector.

What makes a successful government organization? A study investigating successful government and private organizations was recently conducted by the Workforce Effectiveness and Development Group (WED) of the Office of Personnel Management (OPM). The selection of ten successful organizations was based on three major criteria: (1) the organization produced a good or well-respected product; (2) the organization appeared to be a good place to work; and (3) the organization was sound or healthy and had been so over a sustained period of time. The organizations chosen for the study were:

Arena Stage (Washington, D.C.)
City of Charlotte (Charlotte, NC)
City of Sunnyvale (Sunnyvale, CA)
Dana Corporation (Toledo, OH)
Hewlett-Packard (Palo Alto, CA)
L. L. Bean (Freeport, Maine)
Time, Inc. (New York City, NY)
U.S. Customs Service (Washington, D.C.)
U.S. Forest Service (Washington, D.C.)
U.S. Passport Service (Washington, D.C.)

WHAT MAKES A SUCCESSFUL GOVERNMENT ORGANIZATION?

Based on data gathered from a series of structured interviews, observation, and written organizational materials, the following characteristics of successful organizations were drawn.

Organizational objectives are well established, clearly understood, and widely supported within the organization.
The organization is perceived to be special in some way, either in its product or in how it operates. A feeling of pride in the organization exists.

Management is strongly people oriented. Individuals receive fair and respectful treatment. The atmosphere is friendly and informal.

Managers emphasize innovative people management but don't feel their organizations are particularly innovative in terms of their product.

Delegating responsibility and the authority to carry it out are considered essential to motivation.

Performance goals are clearly understood and mutually agreed upon; successful performance is recognized.

Organizational communication is regarded as the weak link, even though other organizational characteristics are rated high.

The authors of the study also listed a compendium of the basic management principles characterizing successful organizations that are worth mentioning:

1. Delegation of authority and responsibility

- Delegate authority and responsibility to the lowest possible level.
- Give people a job to do, but don't bury them with details.
- Encourage people to ask questions.
- Establish overall goals, but give people a chance to make mistakes. People must be able to see their successes and failures.
- Involve people by keeping them informed.
- Learn to communicate, and especially to listen. Recognize that ultimately you have to get the work done through people.

2. Trust and integrity

- Trust your own people.
- Treat people with respect and dignity, the way you, yourself, would like to be treated.
- Be extremely honest with employees.
- Demonstrate a sense of awareness and concern for others.
- Demonstrate a commitment, on the part of management, to the highest ethical and moral standards.
- Be consistent and set an example in everything you do.

3. Objectives and mission

- Organizational objectives should be realistic, clearly understood by everyone, and reflect the organization's basic character and personality.

- Employees must feel that their organization has a mission, and that they are helping to accomplish that mission.
- Help people understand what their objectives are, and make sure that they have the tools, guidance, and freedom to do their jobs.
- Make individual goals high, but attainable.

4. Challenge and enthusiasm

- Operate with a lean staff. People need to be challenged with plenty of work.
- Offer people new challenges and experiences whenever possible.
- Ensure that their jobs are as interesting as possible, within the task.
- Generate enthusiasm at all levels. Managers should not only be enthusiastic themselves, but must also foster enthusiasm in others.
- Inspire people.
- Be willing to take risks.

5. Employee development

- Make a commitment to train and develop people.
- Help people recognize their own capabilities.
- Promote from within whenever possible. When you hire from the outside you learn only a person's strengths. When you have worked with a person you know strengths, as well as weaknesses.

6. Performance

- Be hard-nosed with poor performers. Have the courage and conviction to remove the poor performer who doesn't respond.
- Raise poor performance issues immediately. There is a natural tendency to avoid conflict, but confronting an individual after initial instances of poor performance have been ignored, will be much more difficult.
- Don't concentrate your efforts on the 8 percent of employees who are weak. Then you will spend all your time on rules and regulations, and never realize the potential of the other 92 percent.

7. Openness and informality

- Keep things informal and open and be accessible. Pomp and

ceremony only serve to get in the way.
- Status symbols, dress codes, and formality are things that encumber an organization, and are artificial and extraneous to what the organization really does.
- Have fun.

Rate Your Own Organization

James Gregg (1981) of the Workforce Effectiveness and Development Group (WED) of the Office of Personnel Management (OPM) has developed a short instrument which allows you to rate the quality of your organization.

Using the following chart, rate the quality of your organization on a scale of 3 to 0.

Outstanding = 3 points
Satisfactory = 2 points
Minimally Satisfactory = 1 point
Unacceptable = 0 points

Rating

_____ 1. The mission, goals, and objectives of your organization are clear.
_____ 2. There are carefully developed priorities for the organization.
_____ 3. The organization and its resources are aligned with the priorities and objectives.
_____ 4. The necessary authority and discretion to accomplish the objectives are available.
_____ 5. The necessary resources (manpower, funds, capital) to accomplish the objectives are available.
_____ 6. The necessary time and stability to accomplish the objectives are provided.
_____ 7. There is understanding and good will on the part of those who provide resource and policy support for the organization.
_____ 8. There is quality, leadership, management, and supervision.
_____ 9. There are good processes and techniques for new program development.
_____10. There is commitment of employees to the organization's goals.
_____11. Clear and challenging performance objectives are specified for each employee.

———12. Employees believe that results and performance are the real basis for the rewards provided by the organization.

———13. There is opportunity for employees to fully utilize their ideas and skills and develop themselves in their work.

———14. There is measurement and evaluation of individual performance.

———15. There is measurement and evaluation of organizational performance.

———16. There is measurement of program and mission performance (including client satisfaction).

———17. There is quick and accurate feedback to both employees and management concerning performance.

———18. There are tangible recognitions and rewards for good performance.

———19. Corrective action is taken in the case of poor performance (individual and organizational).

———20. Selection and development of staff is arranged so that people are in jobs that fully utilize their individual strengths and abilities.

———21. Communication within the organization, and between the organization and its clients, is full and open.

———22. There is a sense of trust and security among employees.

———23. There is healthy competition within the organization.

———24. Staff and support service functions are kept small relative to line functions.

———25. Staff and support service functions are held accountable for providing services and support to line functions.

———26. The organization takes special steps to reduce unnecessary or conflicting procedures, processes, or policies.

———27. Employees are provided attractive, safe, and healthy working conditions.

———28. There is an organizational environment which is conducive to constructive change and utilization of new technology.

———29. Research or analysis is conducted to support the future operations of the organization.

———30. The leadership of the organization generates high expectations of accomplishment.

———Total

How to Interpret Your Organization's Score

0–34   Your organization needs new leadership or a shot in the arm (or head) from Congress.

35–54   Major improvements are needed. The organization and its management need diagnosis to pinpoint and begin resolving the problems.

55–74   Your organization is in pretty good shape, but some adjustments or changes are needed in certain areas.

75–90   Your organization is outstanding. How do you do it?

After you've completed the above questionnaire, go back and place a check next to your 1s and 0s. These represent areas for improvement. Work on these areas as soon as you can.

In summary, this chapter has provided you with examples of effective communication-related programs. In addition, characteristics of effective organization were discussed, and you had the opportunity to evaluate your own organization.

REFERENCES

Ewing, B. 1980. Agency-wide productivity—where it starts. *Performance* (December): 1:1–2.

Gold, K. and D. Seifert. 1981. Successful organizations: How they do it. *Performance* (September): 2:6–12.

Gregg, J. 1981. Rate your organization. *Performance* (September): 1:6.

Office of Personnel Management. Workforce effectiveness and development group. *The quality circle program of the Norfolk Naval Shipyard.* Washington, D.C., April, 1981.

Productivity Rises at HUD. *Performance*, September, 1981, 2:6–12.

AFTERWORD

This book was designed for you, the practicing manager in the federal, state, and local government. The suggestions, techniques, and skills recommended are designed to help make you, and your agencies, more effective. As government managers you must often carry the burden of unsubstantiated criticism from the general public. My own experience tells me that you are the real heroes of the government system. I applaud the commitment and dedication, which is often overlooked, and I hope you have found this book useful.

APPENDIX A

EXERCISES

The following set of exercises is presented to give you a chance to test your understanding of and ability to use some of the communication skills presented in this book.

Observing

Remember: Good communication behavior requires that a supervisor give his or her undivided attention to employees as they speak. It requires comfortable eye contact with the employee, and making him or her feel at ease. Also, it requires that the supervisor discuss (verbally follow) and respond to what the employee brings up.

In the exercises below, three situations are presented. Discuss on a separate sheet what the supervisor is doing wrong. After you have responded to all three situations, compare your answers to those presented at the end of the exercises.

Situation 1

Supervisor has invited employee in to discuss his career. Every so often, as they talk, supervisor rustles through some papers on his desk, and then jots down a few words as though he has just thought of something.

Situation 2

Employee: "You know, I feel like I'm just not going anywhere. Whatever I try to do to get ahead doesn't work."

Supervisor: "Well, I don't know what you're worried about. When I was your age, I wasn't even near where you are now. But I just kept plugging away, and finally it paid off."

Situation 3

An employee has come in to the supervisor's office to talk to her about a problem he's been having with another employee:

Employee: I think Howard is a really nice guy, but there are a few things that he has been doing lately that are really bugging me."

Supervisor: "I thought you and Howard were really good buddies. Aren't you both on the same bowling team?"

Questions

Remember: Closed questions can be answered with a yes or no or with a few words. Open-ended questions allow you more opportunity to express thoughts and feelings. With open-ended questions, you are more likely to find out more about what an employee really is thinking. Avoid closed questions. When you are thinking of a closed question to ask, try to change it to an open-ended question before asking it.

In the exercise below, closed questions will be presented. In the space provided, write a corresponding open-ended question that would allow the person who answers, greater freedom to respond.

1. Do you think the new employee is going to work out?
2. Do you dislike the new method?
3. Would you like to transfer to a new section rather than work for Mr. P?
4. Do you think you qualify for that position?
5. Are you going ahead with implementing plan A?
6. Is it so important that project B is finished by the scheduled deadline?
7. Do you think what Leonard did was wrong?
8. Are you going to stop making this kind of mistake?
9. Do you suppose we could get better organized on this project?

Paraphrasing

Remember: Paraphrasing is verbally expressing to the employee, the important part of what he is saying. This response lets the employee know you are trying to understand him or her. If you have misunderstood, it allows for a chance for him or her to correct you. Also, it is a very respectful way to respond.

In the following exercise, ten excerpts of employees' discussions are given. In the space provided, write out a paraphrase for each excerpt. After the completion of each excerpt, compare your answer with that given at the end of the exercises.

Excerpt 1:

"I think too much importance is given to education around here—that a man with experience who really knows how things are operated is just taken for granted, unless he has the education to back him up."

Excerpt 2

A recent college graduate and new employee says:

> "When I first started working here, there was a lot to learn—but now that I've learned it, things are really routine. I wonder sometimes if you couldn't just train a high-school graduate to do these things. Granted, it would take longer to train him, but I bet it could be done."

Excerpt 3

> "I seem to be getting all the difficult jobs around here. Also, anytime something is really hot, and needs to get done right away, it seems to come my way most of the time. Well, I'm not complaining. There have been some really challenging projects, and I learned a lot from doing them, but it doesn't seem to be getting me anywhere."

Excerpt 4

> "It's a real problem. Sometimes, all four people I type for come to me saying, 'this is top priority stuff, I need it typed as soon as possible.'"

Excerpt 5

> "I know you feel that this is the best way of doing the job, but there are a lot of guys who really have found short-cuts for doing it; they don't understand why you insist that it be done in a specific way, but they're afraid to say anything to you."

Excerpt 6

> "I don't know if I should stay here—I know I can't get promoted here, but my kids are in high school, and it would be a hassle for everybody to uproot them—I just don't know."

Excerpt 7

A newly appointed supervisor is discussing his current job situation with you:

> "The only part of the job I really don't get any satisfaction from is the fact that I'm held accountable for the actions of other people, and knowing that you can't control people—only to a certain extent—that they abide by certain rules and regulations—but when it gets down to the fact you want them to do something, and how accurately they're going to do it . . . I'm not only held accountable for my work—but I'm also held accountable for theirs."

Excerpt 8

"Have you ever noticed how so many people come in late so often? I think if they are going to be paid for a full day's work, they ought to be here on time, like I am."

Excerpt 9

A woman employee says:

"I don't know if you are aware of this, or if maybe you've been trying to protect me, knowing that I have a family, but I've not been asked to go to a single out-of-town conference; all the others in the section have been to at least a couple over the past two years."

Reflection of Feelings

Remember: A reflection of feelings is a response that identifies the feelings the employee is expressing, behind what he or she may be saying. Before you are able to identify a feeling, you must first notice the other person expressing it. This is a skill that requires paying attention to, and observing other people.

In the following exercise, ten excerpts of employees' discussions are given. In the space provided, write out a reflection of feelings for each excerpt. After the completion of each excerpt, compare your answer with that given at the end of the exercises.

1

A new employee has been working in your section for a month. You ask him how he's getting along. He responds:

"I don't know. Something must be wrong with me. Hardly anyone has bothered to speak with me or get to know me, and I haven't been asked out to lunch with anyone."

2

"I've finally had it with that new guy. He is really a pain. I can't tell him a thing. He won't take my advice on how to do anything, and so all the defects he causes come right back to me. I have had all I can stand with that————."

3

"I don't know what people expect of secretaries. 'Do this, do that' all day. I can't even go out of the room for a minute without somebody complaining, and asking me where I've been. We're people too."

4

"I've tried to propose suggestions to him so many times, and I thought they were good ones; he didn't even bother to respond to them, or if he did, he said that we're not ready for that."

5

"I was really looking forward to getting that job I applied for in California. My wife was looking forward to moving back home—it's been a big let down."

6

"You know that proposal I completed yesterday? I don't want to pat myself on the back, but I'm really excited about it. I think they're really going to do something with it. Boy, wouldn't that be something?"

7

"You know, I can't present this paper to the conference group tomorrow. Do you know who will be there? There are a lot of people who could do a much better job than I."

8

"You're always telling me to do more things around here and to take more initiative. I'd like to know what you do around here, besides give orders to other people?"

9

"I'm really trying to learn this work—but Mary tells me to do it this way, and Linda tells me no, her way is the right way—what am I supposed to do?"

SOLUTIONS

Observing

The following answers are discussions of what is wrong with the supervisor's handling of each situation.

Situation 1
Supervisor is maintaining poor eye contact with the employee. From his

activity, it is obvious to employee that supervisor's mind is on something else. The supervisor should be giving employee his undivided attention.

Situation 2
The supervisor is not responding to what the employee has said. He is not showing the employee that he is attempting to understand him, but rather is talking about himself.

Situation 3
The supervisor is not responding to what the employee has said. She is offering her own knowledge about the relationship, and is asking the employee to discuss that. While this may be appropriate later, it is definitely not appropriate at the beginning of the discussion.

Questions

The following are open-ended questions that correspond to the closed questions presented in the exercise.

1. How do you think the new employee will perform?
2. What do you think about this new method? or What do you dislike about this new method?
3. What are your thoughts about transferring to a new section and no longer working for Mr. P?
4. In what ways do you think you qualify for the promotion?
5. What do you intend to do about plan A?
6. What are the consequences of project B not being finished by the scheduled deadline?
7. How do you feel about what Leonard did?
8. How do you think you may be able to improve in that _____ (specify area).
9. What could we do to get better organized on this project?

Paraphrasing

The following responses to the excerpts are appropriate paraphrases of what the employee has said.

Excerpt 1
You feel, perhaps, your experience is not recognized enough, partly because you don't have a degree.

Excerpt 2
Things are getting to be routine for you, and you're wondering if you are being given a chance to put all your education to use.

Excerpt 3
It seems to you that all the difficult and hot projects come your way, but that you're getting no recognition for doing them.

Excerpt 4
It's impossible for you to know just what to give priority to, when everyone wants their typing done immediately.

Excerpt 5
Maybe you would like me to discuss their ideas with them, and give them a chance to do it their way.

Excerpt 6
You are trying to weigh the consequences of staying versus transferring.

Excerpt 7
You don't feel comfortable being responsible for the quality of work your people do.

Excerpt 8
You think that more people should be as punctual as you.

Excerpt 9
Perhaps you think I've neglected asking you to go because you have a family and wouldn't want to go anyway.

Reflections of Feelings

The following are accurate reflections of feelings to the excerpts given.

1
It kind of hurts you that everyone seems to be ignoring you.

2
You're really angry with Jim; he's really gotten to you.

3
You feel used—as though you're being treated like a machine.

4

You sound very angry.

5

It sounds as though you're really disappointed.

6

You're really excited about the possibilities of their implementing your proposal.

7

The idea of presenting your paper to that group really is making you anxious.

8

You're quite upset with me—if I give orders to you, I should be doing some things myself.

9

You are really confused by all that's been going on.

APPENDIX B

CASE STUDY/ROLE PLAY

By the end of the first six months on the job, Pat has achieved some considerable standing among the other people in the office. Pat has received an outstanding performance appraisal, has contributed significantly to the work of the office staff, has willingly and imaginatively helped in the organization of various tasks, has a pleasant manner, and is always ready to help others. Pat is always cheerful, punctual to work and to meetings, an informed contributor to discussions and meetings, generally recognized as a leader among fellow workers, and displays every indication of deriving the greatest benefit and success as a member of this agency.

The above was generally true up to about the middle of Pat's seventh month on the job. However, during the last three weeks, Pat has often been absent from work. On the job, Pat has been agressive, sullen, and whenever possible, has been missing deadlines and has shown little interest in the job. Pat tends to decide on solutions to problems prematurely before fully examining all of the situation. Follow-through on decisions is not always accomplished, which often causes problems later. Finally, planning wasn't sufficiently done prior to the implementation of new procedures, causing part of the work to be redone.

By now, the change in Pat is so obvious that it has come to the attention of the supervisor, who instructs Pat to come to the office at a specified time.

The time is now. The supervisor is seated at the desk. There is a loud knock at the door and. . . .

Preparation for the Upcoming Performance Appraisal

- Note the words in the above case which are inferential.
- Using your own work environment for a frame of reference, redo the inferential statements to make them more descriptive.
- Be sure to consider performance standards and job elements. Use your own agency's evaluation form.
- Review the Generic Communication Skills Model. Decide how you intend to approach Pat during the four phases.
- Decide on several questions you might want to ask Pat.
- What do you consider the key performance issues to be?
- What are your expectations regarding Pat's future performance? How would you convey those expectations to Pat?

Role Play (Optional)

After you have completed the above, do the following:

- Form peer groups of three people.
- Assign the letters A, B, and C to each member of the group.
  A is assigned the role of Pat.
  B is assigned the role of the supervisor.
  C is assigned the role of observer. (The observer is to use the Role Play Critique form—Table B.1.)
- Each role play is to take 10 minutes to complete while the observer (C) evaluates the transaction.
- The observer provides 5 minutes of feedback to the supervisor, using the critique form as a basis for the feedback.
- Roles are changed in the following manner:

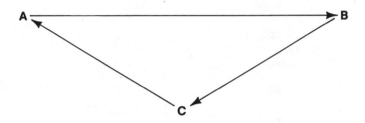

- Time limits for total of three role plays:
  10 minutes for role play
  5 minutes for feedback
  5 minutes for preparation for next role play
  ⎯
  60 minutes total time allotted

TABLE B.1   Role Play Critique—Comments

Skill	Comments	Needs work	Acceptable	Effective	Exceptional
Contact					
Opening Putting person at ease; conveying verbally/nonverbally, genuine, positive regard; setting climate, defining expectations					
Exploration					
Questioning Asking appropriate, nondefense engendering, open, clarifying, & closed questions					
Active Listening Demonstrating interest by paraphrasing feelings, meaning, nonverbal responding, and summarizing					
Specificity Being concrete in feedback, and getting the employee to be specific regarding feelings, experiences, and behaviors.					
Immediacy Discussing your immediate feeling or reaction to the present situation					
Self-Disclosure Sharing previous experiences and observations with the employee					
Confronting Presenting the employee with inconsistencies or illogical conclusions in his/her behavior or thinking—Done tentatively					
Resolution					
Problem Starting Getting the problem openly stated and defined, so it can be dealt with					
Action Planning Developing mutual action plans, and clear future performance expectations					
Disengagement					
Closing Focusing on the demonstrated strengths of employee, and acknowledging their part in the discussion					

INDEX

(Abbreviations: the letter *n* after a page number indicates a reference note; *t*, a table)

ACTION, 3*t*
Action plans, 36, 76
Action verbs, using, in performance appraisals, 61
Administrative Conference of the United States, 3*t*
Administrative Office of the United States Courts, 3*t*
American Battle Monument Commission, 3*t*
Appalachian Regional Commission, 3*t*
Architect of the Capitol, 3*t*
Associative meaning. *See* Meaning, connotative vs. denotative
Attention, importance of, in communication, 16. *See also* Listening, active
Audience, identifying one's, 96
Audio presentations, 100
Autonomy, importance of, in job satisfaction, 45

Baldridge, Secretary, guidelines for clarity in writing of, 24–26
Beavin, J. H., 20*n*
Bell Systems, 95
Behavioral Engineering Systems Training. *See* B.E.S.T. program
Benne, K., 82, 91*n*
Berman, S. I., 13, 20*n*
B.E.S.T. program (HUD), 106–107, 108*t*–109*t*
Board for International Broadcasting, 3
Body language, 16, 69–71. *See also* Communication, nonverbal; Listening, active
Brainstorming, 10, 36, 91
Briefings, effective, steps to, 96–100
Brooks, W., 20*n*
Budget(s)
  cuts, federal, and productivity levels, 32, 103–104
  salary and expense vs. program, 4
Bureaucratese. *See* Jargon, avoiding
Bureaucrats, government, 92–93, 94

Campbell, A. K., 94, 102*n*
Career counseling, giving, 10
Career development survey, GAO, 77–78
Charts, use of, in briefings, 99
Chicota, M., 37, 48*n*

Chronological order, of briefing material, 97
Civil Aeronautics Board, 3*t*
Civil servants, career, 1, 4–5
  power of, 11–12
Civil Service Reform Act, 52–53, 55
Coaching (one's subordinates), 75–78
Commission on Civil Rights, 3*t*
Commission of Fine Arts, 3*t*
Commitment, employee, 32, 33, 34
Commodity Futures Trading Commission, 3*t*
Communication. *See also* Body language; Grapevine
  difficulty of, 14–15
  formal, 28–32
  informal, 27–28
  interagency, 92–102
  interpersonal, 11
  intraorganizational, 34–35
  intrapersonal, 11
  laws of, 1, 10–15
  motivation and, 41
  nonverbal, 1, 2, 15–20
  organizational, 11
  public, 11, 91–102
  small-group, 11
  written, 22–27
Communication climate, 32–40
Communication Climate Inventory, 33–35
Communication skills, improving, 21–50, 95, 107
Community Services Administration, 3*t*
Complaints, communicating, 10
Confronting, 76
Congressional Budget Office, 3*t*
Congress of the United States, 3, 4
Consultative style of leadership, 46, 48, 49
Consumer Product Safety Commission, 3*t*
Contact (coaching/counseling), 75, 76
Contingency approach to leadership, 46, 48, 49
Copyright Royalty Tribunal, 3*t*
Corporations, government, 3*t*
Cost Accounting Standards Bureau, 3*t*
Council of Economic Advisers, 3*t*
Council on Environmental Quality, 3*t*
Council on Wage and Price Stability, 3*t*
Counseling (one's subordinates), 51, 75–78
Cover sheets, use of, on memos, 23
Credibility
  improving one's, 40–41
  perceived, of one's supervisor, 38–39

129